Report Writing

The form and style of
efficient communication

A. E. Darbyshire

 Edward Arnold (Publishers) Ltd

Printed in Great Britain by
Whitstable Litho, Whitstable, Kent

Preface

This book sets out to give a simple and straightforward account of the main principles of report writing, and the chief ways of dealing with them, for those people engaged in science, technology and the business of getting on with the necessary day-to-day jobs of industry.

The author's experience of many years, both among samples of technical literature and among scientists and technologists who have to produce written accounts of their work, has convinced him of three facts. The first is that, on the whole, writing does not present itself as a very congenial task to such writers. The second is that in the production of technical writing there is a great deal of waste and inefficiency. And the third is that the standard of English in the writing thus produced is not very high. Although reports have to be written, either because the daily work of the world cannot be done without them or because research has to be recorded, the writers, it seems, would usually rather do something else, believing that writing is an extraneous chore. The result is that the job is done quickly and hurriedly, very often under pressure, and without a considered appreciation of all the linguistic principles involved. And indeed, the writer of a report is not a free man who can always express himself with the creative liberty that is allowed to other kinds of writers. He is limited by his terms of reference and by the wishes and needs of his readers. The author assumes that the report writer is not a free creative artist in this sense, and accepts that the task of writing reports is probably secondary to the work which demands them. Nevertheless, reports have to be thought of as an essential part of communications in industry, since they embody both records of the facts of that work and of the thinking behind it.

It is hoped that this book will be useful in courses in communication and report writing in further and higher education, and that it will help students generally who are studying scientific and technological subjects in colleges of technology and in universities. The author has in mind courses such as those for Higher National Certificates and Diplomas in science and in the various branches of engineering, courses for examinations for the endorsement of such certificates or diplomas, and the short courses in communication which are nowadays often held in industry and outside.

A.E.D.

Contents

Chapter one:
What is a Report?

1.1 Definition

A report is a written document produced as a result of procedures undertaken to reveal information.

That sentence can be said to be one way of defining the word
report. There can, of course, be many other ways. The most
important part of that way of giving a definition of the word
—and the most important fact that can be said about report
writing—is that which suggests that the purpose of a report is to
reveal information. A report is a document which tells something
definite to its readers, and it does so simply because those who
are going to read it have asked for it to be prepared with just
that intention in mind. The potential readers of a report are
aware of a state of affairs about which they are not as fully informed as they would like to be. They must have further information
if they are going to do their work properly. They have neither the
time nor the special qualifications needed to find out this information for themselves. So they employ someone else to get
it for them. The report should be a statement of what this
information is. Sometimes, in addition, it contains an account
of the way in which the report writer discovered the information, as well as other facts which may be of interest to the
readers, or to some of them.

The word *report* is derived from the Latin prefix *re-*, which
means 'back', and from the Latin word *portare*, which means

'to carry'. A report, therefore, is something which is brought or carried back. Somebody is sent to make an inquiry and comes back carrying the answer. In present-day English, the word has come to imply that what is brought or carried back is factual information.

When we say that a report is produced as the result of procedures, we mean that before a report can be made certain activities have to take place, and that these activities can be described by some such word as *research* or *investigation*.

In some cases it may be part of the report writer's normal duties to supply periodic reports for his employers on work he is engaged to do. Journalists, for instance, are sent out to make inquiries on all manner of topics and to write reports on what they have discovered. This book, however, is not about journalism, for that is a specialized profession, and journalists are professional writers who learn their trade in a special way. The important fact about the work of journalists is the writing itself, for they are writers before they are anything else. But we are concerned in this book with those kinds of people who, engaged on other work which they consider their main source of income, do not want to make writing their daily profession and labour, but do occasionally have to produce written reports for their employers or for those in authority.

This is the case with those who work in the research and development departments of some firms, or those in laboratories and research establishments whose inquiries need to be written up in progress reports of completed tasks. People such as these often tend to believe that the research on which they are engaged is their main job, and that the writing of reports is secondary. This may be so. Certainly such people are employed on the research because of their special qualifications for doing it. Nevertheless, the reports have to be written, and a reliable record of the work has to be made, for there are many other people, who do not have these special qualifications, but who none the less need to know what is going on and what kinds of results are being achieved. In other cases, the report writer's main duties do not always commit him to the regular production of reports. He may take on the role of report writer only temporarily, when he may now and then have to undertake some investigation into some problem, and this would have to be recorded by its being embodied in a report. It is for such a person that this book is chiefly intended.

Perhaps also there may be two other kinds of potential readers. First, there may be students in universities and colleges of technology, studying scientific and technological subjects, who will have sooner or later to learn about report writing. They might as well learn in what the author of this book believes is a reliable way, and not simply be left to pick up the knowledge as best they can. Second, there are the people at the top who ask for the reports—those people who want the information that reports can give them. Such executives should know about report writing so as to know what kinds of document to ask for, and thus be able to influence those under them in the production of well-written reports.

No matter why a report has to be prepared, the same underlying principles will always apply. The writer receives from someone in authority a brief, or set of instructions, which sets out terms of reference and states what he has to investigate and report on. The writer of a report is normally qualified, either by his special training or because of his place in the organization that employs him, to undertake the particular kind of inquiry allotted to him. How he goes about collecting the information for the report will depend on the circumstances. The writer may have to make visits and interview people. He may have to consult libraries and other places where information is stored. He may have to spend hours in a laboratory making tests and noting results. He will certainly have to make notes and prepare written material, and may perhaps have to produce graphs, tables of statistics, drawings, photographs, and sometimes even specimens of materials or models. And how he goes about all this will depend upon what it is precisely that he wants to find out and present to those who will read his report. His methods will be dictated by his own special knowledge and training. They might be dictated by the terms of reference. Familiarity with similar situations in the past may tell the report writer what to do. Or he may have to use his initiative and devise his own set of procedures to deal with a particular case. But the request for a report implies that the writer is expected to make inquiries so that he can set out the required facts.

The definition which we gave also said that a report was a written document. The word *document* is used here in its original sense of 'that which supplies evidence'. This means that a report is a piece of writing which should guide its readers to an understanding of the grounds on which they should hold a certain opinion or opinions. Whether or not they do hold such an opinion or opinions after reading the report is a different matter; but if a report does give its readers grounds for holding an opinion, it gives them evidence based on facts. And facts are not always easy to deal with. Most people find it easier to write about their feelings about facts rather than the facts themselves. That is why a report has to be well written, and to give a properly organized form to the information which it presents.

1.2 Readership

Although in practice it most often happens that a single individual in authority asks for a report to be written, and decides what it shall be about and who shall write it, the readers are likely to be many. For the information that a report provides is normally needed for decision-making and subsequent action. And in making decisions and taking this subsequent action many people are likely to be involved.

No firm or organization can stand still. It moves forward in a constant state of activity, always changing and developing, with something always happening. Good management is partly the guiding of all this activity in a positive direction, so that the people engaged in it are clear about the meaning of what they are doing and the goal which they are trying to reach. Report writing plays a part in good management, because it is a way of supplying information in an accurate form to those people who can make the decisions which control the meaning and direction of the activity of the firm or organization.

The report writer's problem is to present what he has to say so that it can all be made clear to different readers who are likely to read his report for different reasons and from different points of view. Some will read only hastily and superficially, and may miss out parts in which they are not interested or about which they are not qualified to make pronouncements at meetings. Some may want only the general idea of what the report is about and the main conclusions. Others may pay a great deal of attention to the whole, and read every word with minute care. Others may not be able to understand, say, the purely technical details of what the report is about, but may merely want to know, say, the cost of what is involved, or what time and manpower may be needed if the report is accepted. Others again may be so immersed in the technical details that they can think of nothing else.

The report writer has to be able to reconcile these, or similar, conflicting interests. And the only way in which he can do this is by learning how to be detached. It is very easy for a man engaged in some kind of investigation, sometimes over a long period of time, to become so wrapped up in what he is doing that he forgets other people do not see the problem in the same way as he does. At every stage, therefore, in the writing of the report, the writer must pause and review what he has done, and try to imagine the potential readers. What may be obvious to the writer may be completely obscure to one kind of reader; steps in an argument that one reader may understand easily may not be at all clear to another; no two readers are likely to share all the same background knowledge; and sometimes questions of feeling and tone may be important because of the preconceptions and prejudices which some people may bring to what they read.

It follows from this that a report is a written document which has special characteristics which make it different from other kinds of written documents. What chiefly distinguishes a report from other kinds of writing is the purpose for which it is read. A man may pick and choose among the novels which he wants to read for his relaxation or entertainment, or when he sits down to look at a newspaper he can easily decide not to bother with a particular item if it does not interest him. This is not so with a report. The reading of reports is a job which many men have to do in the course of their work; it is represented to them as a duty, and although they may prefer to play golf or linger longer over their lunch than they should, the report has, sooner or later, to be read; and the reader may be compelled to study it carefully, perhaps make notes on it, and be prepared to talk about it, or parts of it, at meetings with his colleagues.

The report writer should remember that this is so, and by

means of the careful arrangement of the parts of his report and the high quality of his writing and the clarity of his expression, make the reader's task so much the easier.

1.3 Special Characteristics

Every report is a special and unique document, arising out of a set of specific circumstances and written by a particular individual for a particular purpose. It is not always possible, therefore, to lay down rules which apply to every case, and no one could foresee all the states of affairs which might call for a report.

Nevertheless, to speak generally, there are three qualities or characteristics which make reports rather different from many other kinds of written documents. The first of these, and probably the most important, is objectivity. That is to say, the report writer's main task is to set down the relevant facts, all the relevant facts, and nothing but the relevant facts, without regard to his personal feelings or views about them. Sometimes, he will be asked to make recommendations, and if he is, then he will have to find good reasons for making them, and the best of such good reasons can only be facts. For a report, as we have said, is a document which provides evidence on which decisions will be based and as a result of which action may be taken. The report writer has to know what evidence is and what it is not. Generally speaking, it can be said that only hard facts can be the basis for decision-making—the factual answers, for example, to questions beginning with *what, where* and *when,* if such answers state quite definitely things or events, places or times.

Secondly, a report, if it is well prepared and produced, is likely to have a distinctive form. We shall later discuss in some detail this question of form, since it is an important one, but it can be said here that the form of anything is its shape, or arrangement of parts, which can make it easily recognizable for what it is. There is a typical arrangement of parts of a report which make it characteristically a report and not anything else. This kind of arrangement makes it easy for readers to find their way about; it gives them clear indications where to look for what interests or concerns them most. In some organizations there is an insistence on all reports being written according to a special formula—heading, aim, summary, introduction, statement of procedures, findings, recommendations—or something like that. This is in order that the readers of the reports can easily learn such a formula and therefore know where to find any particular kind of item that they may want. But to lay down and insist on a rigid formula is perhaps going a little too far. It restricts the writer's freedom unnecessarily, and those who make such rigid demands to standardize procedures (except at the lowest levels of the firm or organization) forget that the occasion for each report is an individual one, and that for different reports different approaches are needed by the writer.

Thirdly, a report should have a characteristic style. Again, this is a question which we shall discuss in more detail later on. The concept of style is a difficult one for many people to grasp who are not professional writers, or whose training has not for the most part been a literary one. But style is the effect of writing on the reader, and is simply language considered from the point of view of the use to which it is put. A bad style is an inappropriate one. A good style is one that does efficiently the job it is asked to do. Different kinds of writers produce different kinds of styles according to the circumstances in which what they are writing is composed. If the report writer understands his job properly, he will normally find the right style for his report arises naturally from his objectivity and the form. Style is a function of language use. In a report, facts have to be expressed for their own sake, within the limits of certain restrictions which the form imposes, and the style should be the most suitable for this expression of fact. This means that the writer should concentrate more on what he is saying than on his way of saying it. But it does not mean that the report writer should ignore accepted refinements of style. It is assumed that he is an educated man and will come to his job equipped with a reasonably sound knowledge of the main points of grammar, an acquaintance with the principles of sentence structure, and a general awareness of what is appropriate to good writing.

These three characteristics, objectivity, form and style, distinguish a good report from a bad, or a civilized way of stating information from an uncouth one.

1.4 Kinds of Reports

Many attempts have been made to draw up lists of all possible types of report. American writers are especially prone to padding out their treatises on report writing with such lists. One comes across formal reports and informal ones, decision reports, pre-decision reports, interim reports, routine reports, test reports, sales reports, executive reports, lower-echelon reports, follow-up reports, valuation reports, inspection reports, operational reports, development reports, customer's reports, and so on—there is no end to the silliness of some people in trying to raise an ordinary, everyday activity into an exact science. Writers have also tried to devise various methods of classifying reports according to their usefulness, their origin, their aim, their subject-matter, their value to the organization, or the level in the hierarchy of the firm in which they operate.

Most people taking up report writing will understand that different circumstances may call for a different type of report. A report is a use of language, and every use of language arises out of a particular situation which dictates that use. If the report writer approaches his task by thinking more of what he is asked to do than how many kinds of reports there are, he is likely to be more successful. For it must be assumed that the writer knows what he is doing, that he knows why he is writing the report, for whom he is writing it, and the kinds of procedures he must undertake in order to find the facts that will make it worthwhile. If he knows that, he knows enough.

Chapter two:
What is Communication?

2.1 Communication

Whatever else a report might be, it is clearly some kind of communication, since it carries a message from the writer to its readers. It might be as well, therefore, to discuss and perhaps clarify some of the main principles of communication before we go on to talk about report writing in more detail.

The word *communication* can be defined as 'the transference of information from one system to another'. In this definition we use the word *system* to give the greatest possible generality, for communication can exist at a number of levels. There is, for example, the genetic communication by which information is passed from parent to offspring by means of amino acid codes, so that the structure of the offspring is specified by a kind of blueprint, as it were, which is transmitted at the time of conception. Animals can communicate among themselves—bees, for instance, by a form of dancing and transmission of smells, or wolves by the movements of their bodies, or birds by quite a large range of methods such as their songs, bodily movements, displays, and even preliminary nest-building behaviour. Human beings, however, have developed the largest known range of means of communication: it not only includes speech and writing, but also a vast repertoire of signalling devices from primitive drumbeats in the jungle or smoke signals in the desert to the sophistication of art and literature and systems of telecommunications extending all over the Earth and even beyond into space. Human beings are also able to construct machines of which parts can be said to communicate with one another.

2.2 Communication Channels

If communication is the transference of messages from one system to another, there must be some kind of vehicle or device by means of which the transference is made. Such a device is normally referred to as a communication channel, which can be represented by the following model:

Encoder→Transmitter→SIGNAL→Receiver→Decoder.

We can apply this, in an ideal way, to human communication by means of language—say, a speaker talking to a listener. The encoder is the speaker's central nervous system, which initiates the transference of the message by choosing from a code a number of signs which can symbolize the content of the message. These signs can exist, first, as what can be called (for want of a more detailed explanation) thoughts or ideas which are, presumably, in that central nervous system. The encoder is able to translate these thoughts or ideas into speech by means of his vocal organs, which, in this example, become the transmitter. This transmitter causes a series of patterns of speech sounds to travel for a short distance through the atmosphere, where they form, during the short period in which they exist as sound waves, the signal. This signal is received by the organs of hearing of the listener who perceives the form of this pattern of successive sound waves, and it is thus caused, by the transmission of nervous impulses from ears to brain, to affect the listener's central nervous system in some way or another. If the listener understands the message, it is because the pattern of sound waves instructs him to select items from the same code as the encoder used before transmitting the signal, and the arrangement of these items embodies the message for him.

In communication in writing the same kind of series of events occurs, and the only differences are that the process of transmission is the making of the marks of a script on some such substance as paper, and that the process of receiving is performed with the eyes.

It should be clear, so far as linguistic communication among human beings is concerned, that during the message's passing across the communication channel the signal is of supreme importance. If we want to study communication in a scientific way, the signal is obviously the most readily available source of trustworthy data. We cannot enter very easily the central nervous systems of encoders and decoders to observe what is going on there, for man's knowledge of neurology is not as yet sufficiently advanced to enable him to give an adequate description. We can, it is true, study the physical properties of the vocal organs and the organs of hearing, and indeed a great deal is already known about what is called articulatory and auditory phonetics. But this knowledge can tell us only how messages are sent and received; it cannot give us the most important information that we want about messages—what they mean and what is their significance in human affairs.

Signals in language, however, can easily be studied, because they can be recorded and preserved, and thus set apart for comparison and analysis. Signals always exist in physical form. So far as language is concerned, they exist either as sound waves in the atmosphere or as the marks of a script made on some semi-durable material like paper.

It is true to say that when we examine signals we are examining the physical embodiments and records of communication channels. In this sense, and for most practical purposes, some kind of recorded organization of signals can be said to be a communication channel itself. This book, for instance, can be looked upon, while it is being read, as such a communication channel, for it is a physical device which organizes and controls a number of signals (its chapters, sections, paragraphs, sentences, page numbers, and so on), and which presents them in a particular form. Thus it is a device for transferring messages which originate with the author, or encoder, to the reader, or decoder. A report, too, would obviously be a communication channel of a similar kind.

2.3 Codes, Signs and Information

The words *encoder* and *decoder*, which we have written to stand for the systems at the beginning and end of a communication channel, naturally suggest another word, that of *code* itself.

B

If we examine a large number of communication channels of the same sort—say, a large number of books written in the same language—we shall discover that the signals can be split up into discrete or individually separate parts. We shall discover this because we shall be able to observe a large number of identical physical forms which tend to recur with greater or less frequency. For example, we shall find that the same letters of the alphabet repeat themselves again and again, or we shall find groups of such letters, which we call words, repeating themselves in the same way. This is one of those observations which is so familiar that we sometimes forget its importance.

Eventually, if we tried to make a catalogue of such repeating forms, we should find that there was only a finite number of them, or—to put the idea in another way—that the encoders, or makers of the signals passing across the communication channels, were using a limited repertoire of signs. And this suggests that communication in general might depend on the existence of a code, and that a code might be something made up of a finite number of signs or items. This is so, and communication in human language, which man has made extremely complex in the course of his evolution, depends on a number of different but interrelated codes evolved over a long period.

We can define the word *code* to mean 'a finite set of pre-arranged signs used for making signals'. And we can define the word *sign* to mean 'some physical mark or event which conveys information'. It should be remembered that the word *information* is used here in a special technical sense which we shall explain later.

There are five main different but interrelated codes upon which communication by means of language depends. Within these five codes there are also sub-codes of various kinds which need not concern us here. We shall deal only with the main outlines.

The first, and basic, code of this system of codes is that of speech sounds. Man learnt to use speech as a medium of communication long before he learnt writing, and there were long ages in the history of man when writing was unknown; it is true to say that most of the men and women who have lived have communicated chiefly by means of speech and have not learnt to read and write at all. The human vocal organs can produce a vast number of different sounds, so vast, indeed, that they have never been counted, and so vast, therefore, that if they were all used in human speech human memory would never be able to cope with them. Consequently only a small repertoire of these sounds is used by human beings in speaking all the languages of the world—about a hundred and sixty in all, and not all these sounds are used in all languages. English uses forty-four, and this is a large number when English is compared with some other languages. This code of speech sounds is learnt by normal human beings in the earliest years of childhood.

Second, these forty-four speech sounds are used in different combinations and permutations by speakers to make a code of words. That is to say, different ways of making groups or patterns of some of these sounds produce forms, and all the sounds eventually produce a variety of forms, which are units made of a distinctive arrangement of parts. These forms can thus be differentiated and made recognizable by speakers and listeners as different physical things—as different patterns of sound waves in the atmosphere in the case of speech. All the words of the English language are, when they are spoken, patterns of speech sounds arranged in different ways. Again, the basis of this system of the patterning of the speech sounds of the language is learnt by human beings in the earliest years of childhood.

Obviously, the code of the words of a language is very much larger than that of its speech sounds, and in many cases, as with English, can become so large that no individual speaker can ever be familiar with all of it. Nevertheless, although no speaker knows all the words of English, all speakers know some of them. And some speakers knew more than others, and all the speakers put together know all. Thus all the speakers share a quite large common stock of words which are used in the ordinary everyday communications among people as they go about their normal affairs; and small groups of people, engaged in some particular profession or trade, have a stock of special or technical words which they use in special circumstances. Chemists, for instance, are familiar with a special stock of words which they use in their professional moments, but which are not shared by, say, electrical engineers or deep-sea fishermen, who have their own particular jargons. In this way, among the words of the total code, there develop smaller sub-codes or sets of technical terms and special usages.

Third, there is a grammatical code, which is largely shared by the whole of the English-speaking world. This consists of a set of rules for the use of words, and these rules have been established by convention as the language has developed among its users. Again, the basic needs of these rules are learnt by normal uses of the language during the first years of childhood.

When language is used, its words are arranged in conventionally established patterns we call sentences. Just as speech sounds combine into words, so words can be combined into sentences, which are patterns of classes of words, or which are forms made distinctive by the arrangement of their parts. And again, just as there is a limited number of speech sounds, so there is a limited number of sentence forms. If this were not so, communication in language would be impossible, for communication depends ultimately on the recognition by the decoder of the form of expression which the encoder has chosen. Such recognition can exist only if the encoder makes his choice of items from a code which the decoder already knows about. We have defined a code as a prearranged set of signs, and the word *prearranged* suggests here that both the encoder and the decoder know what the code is. As human beings, we find, all of us, that the prearrangement of the code of language was made before we were born and when, as small children, we learnt how to speak and listen, or use language, we also learnt unconsciously what that prearrangement was.

Fourth, among highly civilized peoples, there is a code of writing. This consists of the items of a script, which, by some prearrangement or other, is made capable of representing and recording the speech sounds of the language. Sometimes, as in Chinese or the language spoken in ancient Egypt, the marks of the script represent whole words, though it is more common to find, as in European languages, that the marks of the script normally represent, with greater or less efficiency, the basic speech sounds. In present-day English, we use both methods, though we use the second more often than the first. For us, the writing code consists of fifty-two items, which we call the small and capital letters of the roman alphabet, a few punctuation marks, and ten arabic numerals. These have to represent the forty-four speech sounds and the combinations of some of them which are the basis of the English language. Since the small and capital letters can nominally only represent twenty-six sounds, and since some of them sometimes represent the same sound twice, our script is not a very efficient one. The punctuation marks are signs which represent both whole words and the ideas which these words stand for; the symbol *?* stands for the whole words *question mark*, and at the same time indicates in normal usage that the string of words which it follows is arranged in the form of a question. The arabic numerals, such as those used for numbering the pages of this book, are also symbols for whole words. In addition, because ours is a highly complex civilization, we have to supplement the stock of the generally used signs of the writing code with the special symbols of the mathematics and the sciences, which are learnt by some members of society but not all.

Fifth, there is a code of linguistic forms in which it is possible to observe differences in the arrangement of parts in sustained discourses. These differences arise because of the function in society of the particular kind of discourse, and a specific form makes recognition by decoders much easier. The basic material of the language is taken and shaped in different ways by different users because these different users do not want the resulting language uses to do the same things. They want to cause different effects on different listeners or readers, because language uses arise in different social circumstances and have a variety of purposes. Thus we can easily see that there grow up in society various kinds of language uses which acquire special characteristics of form according to the uses to which they are put. A cookery recipe, for instance, has a specialized and characteristic arrangement of parts which makes its form different from that of, say, a love story in a woman's magazine; or a meteorologist producing a weather forecast uses a different method of employing the resources of the language from those used by writers of Acts of Parliament; we do not expect to find a detective story or a spy thriller written in the same way as a textbook of electrical engineering; people do not write advertisements for the personal column of *The Times* in the same way as they write legal documents; and so on. In this way, various kinds of language uses become institutionalized, applicable only to specific occasions and often to specific kinds of people. The printed instructions about installing gas-fired central-heating equipment, for instance, may be understood quite easily by the gas fitters who do the installing, but completely incomprehensible to the person in whose premises the equipment is installed.

Each of these five different but closely interrelated codes can be said to be a set of signs. Speech sounds are signs; words are signs; sentences are signs; the items of a script are signs; and the ways in which language is used are signs. Some of these signs, of course, are, or can be, used as if they were signals as well, that is, the physical embodiments of whole messages. It is possible to think of occasions when a single speech sound could be the embodiment of a whole message. A single word—for example, 'Private' painted on a door—could convey a complete message; and a sentence—such as 'Keep off the grass'—could do the same; while most of us at some time or another have used single letters of the alphabet as a means of identifying something—in a building where the writer of this book sometimes works three wings are called N, E and S (north, east and south), and these letters are enough to identify them to other users of the building.

If a sign is a physical mark or event that conveys information, then it is so, and it does so, because of its form. The only way in which one can identify any one of the three letters N, E and S, for instance, is in the fact that the particular one identified has a different shape from the other two when it is written, or in the fact that the words *en*, *ee* and *ess* each make different patterns of sound waves in the atmosphere when spoken.

The process of communication is a continual selection and rejection of signs. These acts of selection and rejection are made possible only by the forms of the signs. It is only the forms of the signs which can tell encoders and decoders which to select and which to reject, because the forms are the only means of identification and recognition. When an encoder wants to send a message he chooses certain signs from the appropriate code and rejects others. These chosen signs he assembles into the signal by making them into a pattern of signs which is also a sign itself. When the decoder comes to interpret the signal, this form or pattern of signs tells him what kind of signal it is, and the signs that make up the signal tell him to choose from the same code the same signs as the encoder used, so that both can have an identical conception of what the signal is. The signal is merely a device for instructing the decoder to make the same selection from the code as the encoder made.

The information which a sign carries, in the technical sense of the word *information*, is thus an instruction to select. And since a code is by definition a prearranged set of signs, communication consists in obeying these instructions conveyed by the signs of the signals.

It should be clear from this discussion that the concept of form is a very important one in the understanding of communication in language, because the form of a signal is an essential clue to its meaning, and the meaning of what passes across a communication channel is, in practice, what most people normally want to know.

To speak generally, we can say (without going too far into the details of philosophical linguistics) that the meaning of a sign—and also, therefore, the meaning of a signal—is what it refers to. This expression 'what it refers to' here begs a number of questions. But in order to be fairly simple we can say that what a sign or a signal refers to in the first place is an idea or concept in the mind of the encoder. Such ideas or concepts can be of two kinds. They can be purely mental concepts, such as the abstractions of logic, mathematics or science—as when, for instance, we speak of such concepts as absolute zero, or the square root of minus one, or moment about a point—or they can be ideas of things in the universe outside the mind—as when a man slaps his hand on his desk and says 'This desk at which I am sitting now'. So a signal could be said to refer to a concept thought up and constructed inside the mind or to an object or event outside the mind. In the second place, 'what the signal refers to' can become what the decoder thinks about or imagines when he has interpreted it; if he interprets the signal correctly, then for him it refers to the same concept or idea as that which existed in the mind of the encoder when the message was sent.

In this way, we can think of meaning as an activity. It is a way of responding to a stimulus. When an encoder constructs a signal out of the signs of a code, he hopes he will make something physical—a pattern of sound waves in the atmosphere, or the pattern of the marks of a script on paper—and he hopes, too, that this physical thing will be a stimulus to the decoder who will respond by thinking about the same idea or concept as the encoder was thinking of. If this identity of views is established, then communication has taken place. We can be fairly certain, one imagines, that complete identity of views is very rare indeed, and that the best to be hoped for in most circumstances is a close approximation.

Normally, it is the responsibility of the encoder, who is the initiator of the message, so to arrange the signs of the code in the signal that the decoder will respond to them in the proper way, and thus make this approximation as close as it can be made.

2.4 Register

A useful concept employed by students of linguistics, and one that can give a valuable insight into what people do with language, is that of register. We can say that the register of any given sample of language use, which we can observe in the speaking and writing of people engaged in the day-to-day affairs of the world, is the total of the characteristics it acquires as the result of the use to which it is put. This concept of register can be broken down into five components: context, sense, medium, tenor and style.

Every language use arises in the world because some human being causes it to happen. And some human being causes it to happen because normally there is a necessity for it. This necessity may be more or less pressing and urgent according to circumstances. Two housewives having a good gossip in a supermarket are providing a sample of language use, though not a very pressing or urgent one; nevertheless, there are adequate social reasons for their having their gossip. An officer in the heat of battle giving orders to his troops is also providing a sample of language use, and the necessity for such a one as this is clearly very urgent and pressing. But whatever the necessity, the use of the language will arise in some social circumstances, to which, it is supposed, the use will have some kind of reference.

We can refer to the surrounding circumstances in which the language use occurs as the *context*. Such a context may be a state of affairs outside language, but which can provoke language, as, say, an accident, which can cause people to give orders, make telephone calls, produce writing in a policeman's notebook, and lead to a report's being made. Or such a context may itself be a use of language, as, for example, a question which provokes an answer, or the thrust and counterthrust in the making of points in a discussion or debate.

It is clear that the context of a language use will have an effect on its sense. The *sense* of a use of language is what it is about, or what it refers to, or its subject-matter. And in normal circumstances the sense has some relationship or reference to the context. If I go into a tobacconist's shop in order to buy cigarettes, I do not recite a poem, or ask for something that is not likely to be on sale in the shop, or make a speech about some burning political question of the moment. There is a time and a place for all things. Therefore, if the context has an effect on the language use, it will also have an effect on the kind of language used, and the subject-matter or sense will dictate the kinds of words used (they will refer to things or ideas in the context), the sort of sentence structure used (statements, questions or commands, for example—which shall it be?), as well as the length of what is said, the amount of detail gone into, and so on. The amount of language activity will also be dictated by the context and the sense. During a football game, a player's simply shouting 'Here!'—one single word, yet nevertheless a use of the language—may set up the disposition of some of his team that results in the winning goal; but the reporter's account written afterwards to appear in a newspaper of how the winning goal was scored may use many more words.

The context and the sense of a language use will combine to dictate the medium. The *medium* is the way in which the occasion of the language use and the sense organize the linguistic material. Two obvious media are speech and writing. Sometimes the context and the sense will organize the language use through the medium of speech only, for there are many occasions when speech is appropriate and sufficient. At other times they will indicate that what has to be communicated must be written. But within these two great divisions there can be many subdivisions. Uses of language in the spoken medium can range from casual chatter and gossip, through heart-to-heart talks, conversations, interviews, discussions, formal meetings, lectures, sermons, to political speeches and debates that may decide the destinies of nations. And in the written medium there can be all the subdivisions of imaginative literature on the one hand, and all the different kinds of the language of information and instruction on the other—whole libraries of written language, ranging from a number in a telephone directory to the most profound works of philosophy.

The question of medium is a very important one, for two reasons. The origin of the medium of a language use in context and sense imposes on the speaker or writer the responsibility of making a careful choice of how he uses language within that use. And on some occasions the speaker or writer has to be more conscious of what he is doing than on others. There are some occasions when the user of language has to think long and seriously about the kind of language he is using. A group of men having a drink at a bar need not, perhaps, be over-anxious or very self-conscious about their use of language; but put those men in a different situation—say, at a committee meeting—and they would, or should if they were doing their job properly, have to use language with much greater precision and for-mality. An inter-office memo to a colleague who is also a friend could be dashed off in a moment without, perhaps, much thought about the way in which the message was written; but a report to the managing director should need long and careful thought if it is to be effective.

The context, sense and medium of a language use, again, combine to produce what is nowadays called the tenor. The *tenor* of a language use is the way in which the social relation-ships of the participants in the language activity affect the use of the language. All of us, at some time or other in our lives, have been aware of situations in which what we have said or written has been influenced by the intended listener or reader. A candidate at an interview for a job finds himself in a relation-ship with those who are interviewing him which makes him use language differently from the way in which he would use it when talking to his personal friends. Adults talking to children do not always use language in the same kind of way as when they are talking among themselves. We write private letters to friends, girl-friends or wives in a very different kind of language from that which we use in business letters. Expert talking to expert may use language very differently from the way he uses it when talking about the same subject to a layman. Again, this question of tenor can assume an importance in some circumstances in the same way as medium can. For some occasions on which language is used are clearly more serious occasions than others, and therefore call for a more responsible attitude on the part of the speaker or writer. This attitude will be dictated, on every occasion, by the register that should be appropriate to the circumstances in which the speaker or writer finds himself.

All these four aspects of register—context, sense, medium and tenor—combine to form the style of the language use. In this way, we can see that the concept of style is not something esoteric and literary, but something intensely practical. It is something social, a matter of the adaption of the language use to the circumstances in which it occurs. It is also a matter of social necessity, for living in society means making allowances for other people; and that applies to acts of communication as well as to anything else.

Given a great deal of linguistic knowledge, and a background of study in the science of linguistics, it is possible to explain the concept of style scientifically. But such an explanation, of course, is beyond the scope of this book. Nevertheless, style can also become something that is felt and appreciated, if the reader cares to take a little trouble. Style is a quality of the use of language which appears more clearly and obviously in writing than in speech. The reader should therefore try to observe differences of style in various language uses that he can come across quite easily, and he should compare and contrast features of register which he can find in books, magazines and newspapers or any other pieces of writing he can come across. He should look at the kinds of words and sentences, the figures of speech, and the relationships of all these to the subject-matter. For instance, he might compare and contrast a weather report with a cookery recipe, and then both of them with an extract from a novel or a story in a magazine. He might compare a political article in a week-end review with the report of a football match in a popular daily newspaper, or the review of a film with an article in a technical journal, or an extract from the maintenance or operating manual of some machine or piece of equipment with an extract from a book on an utterly different topic. In this way, if he takes the study with some seriousness, he will be able to gain some insight into how language works in different social circumstances.

2.5 Communication and the Report Writer

What is the value of all we have said so far in this chapter for the writer of reports?

In the first place, since a report is obviously something which communicates, an acquaintance with the general theory of communication, however slight, does not seem to be out of place. The idea that a report is one kind of communication channel should lead the report writer to a clearer understanding than he might otherwise have had of what a report is. The knowledge that when he writes he is drawing upon the resources of a code should also help him to clarify his ideas about what he is doing. If he understands what the signs of a code are, and the different ways in which different signs can convey different sorts of information (in the technical sense), he is becoming better acquainted with the tools of his trade, with what they are, and how to use them well. Moreover, in the preparation of reports, the writer will have information (in the non-technical sense) presented to him; and it can be presented to him either through what people say as a result of his questions and their answers, or through written documents which he may have to examine in their entirety or in part. Before he can become an encoder of messages, the writer must become a decoder, and he must learn how to interpret the messages which he receives, how to evaluate their importance, and how to select and reject among them.

In the second place, the notion of register and of the components of which it is made can be of great importance to him in his assessment of what he is doing, both when he is making this preparation and when he comes to write. Every report, as we have said, is the result of some procedures undertaken to reveal information (in the non-technical sense). The context of the piece of writing that is the report is the starting point of these procedures; it is the state of affairs which occasions the report and which therefore dictates its subject-matter. Obviously, the writer must have a clear idea of what his subject-matter is. And the subject-matter will dictate the medium, or the form, of the report, and if the writer is aware of how this happens his awareness of what he is doing will be increased; he will be able to stand back from his work, and see what he is doing in a clear and objective light. Since a report will always have a readership, the question of tenor is obviously an important one. The writer will have to understand what kinds of people he is writing his report for. He will have to bear in mind that not all his readers will have the same kind of knowledge of, or familiarity with, or attitudes towards, the subject-matter of the report as he may have. He may, in some cases, be a technical expert writing for laymen. On the other hand, he may sometimes have to remember that some of his readers, if not all, could be just as expert in the field of the subject-matter as he is, perhaps sometimes even more expert. In any case, these considerations should indicate to him how to assess the facts he has to present and in what form to present them— whether, for instance, some facts should be given in continuous prose at some length, or whether only the main conclusions should be given, or what, for instance, is the relative value of one part of the report when it is thought of in connexion with another part. Sometimes he will have to decide whether some of the facts can be presented by means of tables or graphs, diagrams, plans or drawings, and if so, he should know which facts and why; for such extra-linguistic material can be just as communicative as language.

Such considerations, too, should help the writer with the style of his report. It is through the style that the total effect of the report on the reader will be made; through its style it will be judged, since that is the only way the readers will have of assessing it. The point is, that report writing is an activity which needs the preparation of long and conscious thought. As Humpty Dumpty said to Alice in *Alice through the Looking-glass*, when he was speaking of words, it is a question of who is to be master. The report writer should certainly be master of the means by which he chooses to communicate.

Chapter three:
Preparation and Planning

3.1 Terms of Reference

In this chapter we propose to try to follow through the preparation and planning of an imaginary report from the first intimation that one has to be written to the stage just before the actual writing of it.

Every report starts from a sort of brief, or set of instructions given to the report writer to tell him what to report on. This brief is a statement of what kind of information is wanted by those in authority who ask for the report. Obviously, this brief has to be studied with some care, so that the writer will eventually produce just the kind of report that is wanted, and not any other. The instructions which the writer thus receives are normally called his terms of reference. They give the points, subjects or topics which the writer is to report on, and, because time is limited and the writer could not say everything that it might be possible to say about these points, subjects or topics, they also state particular aspects or parts which he has to refer to. The terms of reference will usually be worded in such a way that the task presented to the writer of the report is clear. When this is the case, all he has to do is to get on with the job, carry out whatever investigations he thinks are necessary, and get down to writing the report.

Sometimes, however, it may happen that things are not so simple as this; and the writer, when he considers his terms of reference, should always look at them carefully for possible snags and difficulties. It may happen that those in authority have not completely evaluated the situation, so that the writer, when he comes to carry out his inquiries, finds that unforeseen problems lie in his path. Those in authority, as we have said, ask for a report because they are not as well informed as they would like to be about a particular state of affairs—if they were, there would be no need for the report. So it is always possible that somebody, somewhere, has failed to see something, to appreciate the existence of a hidden difficulty, to underestimate the seriousness of a problem or the extent of the investigation which the report writer may have to undertake. In such circumstances, the writer may have to go beyond his terms of reference, or may have to bring in material of a kind that was not asked for, or even raise points that those who gave him his instructions had not even thought about. If this should happen, the writer should be quite fearless in drawing attention to it in his report—provided, of course, he explains the relevance of what he is doing and why he has gone beyond what was asked for.

Suppose the report writer is presented with some such terms of reference as:

> To report on the kinds of air pollution likely to be encountered at the site of the proposed new research station buildings at Wilmorton, and the kinds of air-conditioning equipment likely to be required.

Reading through these terms of reference, the writer would—perhaps first of all if he were a man who cared for the English language—note that the words *encountered* and *required* were typical of the kinds of words used in technical and business jargon, and he might ask: why not use the simpler words *found* and *needed*? However, he would dismiss this question with a shrug and a consciousness of his own superiority as a writer of plain English, and pass on to the job in hand.

He would note that the terms of reference fall into two parts—the first dealing with the kind of air pollution likely to be found on the site, and the second dealing with air-conditioning equipment. But he would also notice a connexion between the two parts, namely, that the air-conditioning equipment must deal, when it is installed in the research station buildings, with the polluted air of the site and its neighbourhood. The writer has, therefore, several tasks before him. He has

(1) to find out the possible causes of air pollution;
(2) to find out whether there are any of the air-polluting agents on or near the site and, if so, which;
(3) to find out what kinds of air-conditioning equipment are available; and what the different kinds are capable of doing;
(4) to examine the proposed layout and working arrangements for the research station buildings to find out how, or if, all the rooms in the buildings will be affected by the polluted air.

It is assumed that the terms of reference have been given to the writer, and not to someone else, because he already knows something about air pollution and air-conditioning equipment. But even if he knows nothing about the subject he can easily work out the scheme outlined above. All that is needed is to make inferences from the terms of reference. For the writer of those terms has taken it for granted that the air in the region of the site of the proposed research station is polluted, and that some kind of air-conditioning plant will be needed. Two facts therefore become clear from the reading of these particular terms of reference. The first is that those who call for the report are interested in two things—the kind of air pollution likely to be found in a particular place and the sort of equipment needed to deal with it; this tells the writer precisely what sort of information he is expected to supply, that is, his objective is stated for him. The second fact is that the form of the terms of reference tells him what sort of procedures he must undertake to find out the information he has to supply.

3.2 Preparation and Planning

The schedule of the four tasks which was set out in the previous section represents the report writer's interpretation of the terms of reference that were given to him. He is, in that respect, the decoder of a message, and his first job, therefore, is to make certain that he has interpreted the message correctly. In other words, he has to be conscious of what he is doing.

Once he is sure that his interpretation of the terms of reference is correct, the report writer can proceed with his preparation and planning. These two sets of activities consist of following through the procedures which the terms of reference will dictate. Although the procedures will most often not be stated in the terms of reference, they will nevertheless be implied, and in any case, if the writer's interpretation is correct, he will know what he has to do.

The first question he will have to consider in his preparation and planning is one of time. How long will it take him to prepare and write the report? Sometimes the terms of reference give a date by which, or before which, the finished report must be submitted; and in some cases—as with, for instance, progress reports which are needed for regular committee or board meetings—the date will be known. If a date is given, the report should be submitted by that date; those who have asked for it presumably have good reason for wanting it by then. But it may happen that they do not know how long it will take to finish it. That they have asked for the report shows that they are not completely informed about the subject-matter, and so the writer may find when he sets out to do the job that unforeseen circumstances have to be considered.

The obvious answer to the question, 'How soon after he receives the request for it should the writer submit his report?' is therefore 'As soon as he can, and the sooner the better'. If a date is given, then the report writer should make every effort to comply with it. But if, because of the extent of the investigation, he cannot comply with such a deadline, he will have to say so in an interim report, which will state his progress so far and give the reasons for his not having done all that was asked of him.

The writer should make a timetable of the work he intends to do, planning his investigations so that he works to a system and can check progress against the timetable. Although it is not easy to keep rigidly to such a timetable, the effort should be made so that the work is controlled and the writer can know, or try to assess, at any time how much he has done and what he still has to do.

There may be people whom he will have to interview, books he may have to consult, materials to be tested, experiments to

c

be carried out; and all the time during which these sorts of activities are going on, there will be notes the writer has to make, while the documents he has collected, the tables, graphs, drawings and other materials he may have amassed, will have to be sorted, ordered and evaluated. Some of the material thus collected will be more important than others, and some may turn out to be valueless. It may happen that at the beginning of the investigation some of the material collected may not be properly understood until it is set against material collected later. Sometimes part of the report writer's investigations may lead him up blind alleys; at other times it may lead him to consider new facts which he had not at first envisaged.

All such methods of inquiry will take time, and some of them may even waste it. And as the information is gathered, there will be a continual sifting and evaluation of it, along with the setting aside of apparently irrelevant material, but not the destroying of it, just in case some other material, not yet gathered, shows that it is relevant after all. It will thus be seen that a rigid timetable is bound to be upset as the work proceeds.

The main stages in the preparation and planning of a report are therefore likely to be something like the following:

1. Interpreting the terms of reference.
2. Making a list of the main jobs to be done.
3. Timetabling these jobs with an estimated date or time of completion of each.
4. Collecting the material in accordance with the timetable.
5. Sorting and evaluating the material while it is being collected.
6. Evaluating and arranging the material when all is collected.
7. Drafting, writing and revising the report.

While the material is being collected, as people are interviewed, notes are taken, documents amassed, libraries visited, graphs drawn, tables prepared, illustrations made, and so on, the report writer is learning more and more about the subject-matter of his report, and as he passes from one stage to the next the job of evaluating the material should become easier. While all this is going on the writer is also learning to find his way about among all the documents and notes on the material which he has collected.

Even so, part of the preparation and planning of a report consists of choosing a means of organizing and controlling ways of storing and recording all the information. Each report writer is likely to evolve his own methods, or the methods may sometimes be dictated by the firm he works for. But generally speaking, it can be said that the terms of reference, once they have been correctly interpreted, will dictate the methods themselves. For the correct interpretation of the terms will show the writer what *kinds* of information he will have to collect, so that the material can be classified under the headings of these kinds.

For instance, in the example of the terms of reference given on page 25, and with the list of jobs to be done that was given after them, it will be noticed that the report writer will want at least three kinds of different information. He will want to know something about air pollution in general and about the causes of air pollution on the site in particular. He will want to know something about air-conditioning equipment. And he will want to know something about the proposed building. This will mean that the report writer will want at least three main files of documents, and will naturally want also reference numbers or indexes to the individual documents in each file.

Some writers may prefer to have a simple straightforward filing system; others may like to have a card-index; others, again, may like to have a combination of both. A great deal will depend on the nature of the material that will accumulate as the inquiry proceeds. Sometimes it could consist of just a few notes on a memo pad; sometimes it will be a whole mass of material which will have to be carefully sorted and arranged. For the bits and pieces of paper, and even other material, may come in all sizes and quantities, and the documents, or records of evidence, will vary accordingly. A document could be a short note or even a telephone number scribbled on the back of an envelope; it could be a long letter typed on several sheets of a firm's notepaper; it could be a brochure, a leaflet or a catalogue, a parts list or a maintenance manual the size of a large book; or it could be a bulky map or a set of plans or drawings. And nowadays it is sometimes possible to collect evidence, as at an interview, by means of tape-recordings.

Sometimes, too, not all the documents relating to a particular topic can be collected at once; where a series of tests has to be carried out, for example, the work may take weeks or even months, and the necessary records will have to be assembled slowly and patiently. But whatever the kind of document or the time taken to receive it, the report writer will need some method of classifying his material, and he should be able to find at a moment's notice any document that he may need.

The report writer is left largely on his own in these matters, so that whatever method he adopts is likely to be one that suits him personally. But it is not a bad idea to learn from books on office management and organization how filing systems work, and what help there is to be found in the different kinds of office equipment available. One thing is certain: no matter what filing system or methods of classification may be used, there are always two criteria which will test the report writer's organizing ability. The first is: does it work efficiently? The second is: can its accuracy always be relied on? If the report writer finds that his filing system does not enable him to obtain immediately the information that he wants, or if the information it reveals is inaccurate, then clearly something is wrong with it.

3.3 Collecting the Material

Once the report writer has received his terms of reference, interpreted them correctly, and made some plan, with a timetable, of his intended procedures, he can get on with the job. The ways in which the material for the report may be collected can usually be summed up under five headings:

1. Drawing on specialized and personal knowledge.
2. Research and experiment.
3. Use of libraries and information bureaux.
4. Interviews.
5. Correspondence.

Not all these ways, of course, need to be used in the preparation of every report, and sometimes one or two of them may overlap, but in general they give the main ideas of the principles of collecting material which the report writer might adopt.

If he is presented with the terms of reference given on page 25, it is likely that they have been given to him because he already knows something about the subject. He can therefore immediately draw on his specialized knowledge. Consequently, the instruction which he writes for himself in the list of jobs to be done, 'to find out what types of pollution exist in the air', is perhaps superfluous. Nevertheless, the readers of the report may not have the writer's specialist knowledge, and so the writer should consider carefully whether a statement of what kinds of polluted air exist should appear in his report or not. For himself, he might just write down the three words, 'Dust, aerosols, gases', on a scrap of paper and leave the matter at that, or he might produce a more extensive description of what is meant by dust, aerosols and gases as polluters of the atmosphere.

When he comes to the second of his five tasks, the report writer will clearly have to resort to research and experiment. He will have to visit the site, take samples of the air, and measure the extent, if there is any, of the air pollution. This is the sort of job for which the report writer's special qualifications may well equip him, and it is also the sort of job which may take some time. For the pollution in the atmosphere at the site may very well vary from season to season, or according to the direction of the wind, or be different in wet weather from what it is in dry weather. Consequently, the report writer, or somebody else working under his direction, will have to visit the site with instruments that can measure air pollution, and will have to make tests at various times and during different sorts of weather, so that the kinds of air-cleaning equipment which are eventually to be recommended can be decided upon.

In this connexion, too, it may be necessary for the report writer to visit some library or other to find out if any records have been kept anywhere of the air pollution in the district. Such records are kept, some of them going back for many years, and a knowledge of them could be helpful in showing the tendencies of different sorts of air pollution over a period of time, the effects of smoke abatement bye-laws, the policy of the local authority in dealing with the problem, and so on. We shall give hints later on in this book on the use of libraries, so there is no need to give them here.

The writer of the particular report here being considered may be an expert on air pollution and air-conditioning equipment, but it may happen that he knows nothing whatever of the research station buildings. He has therefore to seek information from somebody who does know. Part of his job will be to go to the architects, for instance, and consult with them. Normally, before any building such as a research station is built, there is, somewhere in somebody's mind the knowledge of why it is going to be built and what it is going to be like. There is also usually in existence what is called a schedule of accommodation. This is a statement of the kind of building to be erected, of the number and kinds of rooms, together with a specification of the particular needs of each room, corridor, staircase, lift-shaft, and so on. Because the writer of this report knows about air pollution and air-cleaning equipment, he may have a great deal of general knowledge, but none which can apply to this particular building until he has seen such a schedule of accommodation.

Interviews with people to find information that may eventually go into a report should be conducted with some care. The interviewer should go to meet, or should receive, the person he is to interview with a very clear idea in his mind of what the interview is for, exactly what kind of information he wants, and what is the minimum of information he can ask for without prejudice to the final contents of his report. He should not waste his own time, nor that of the person from whom he is seeking information; he should therefore prepare a list of questions he wants to ask, perhaps writing them down with one question on each page of a notebook or memo pad, so that he can have plenty of room to jot down notes of the answers. Sometimes a personal interview is followed up when the person interviewed later sends the report writer written information. This may be especially necessary when tables of statistics, plans or drawings are involved; figures, dates, specifications of quantities, measurements, and numerically expressed information generally, should always be carefully checked, and double-checked before it reaches the final report.

It may also be possible to make tape-recordings of some interviews. When this is done, the recording should be played back to those who have taken part in the interview; what is said by word of mouth is never likely to be so carefully worded as what is written and some speakers may want to have second thoughts.

It is good manners to allow them to do so. In any case, a transcript should be made by the person who keeps the tape, and copies of this transcript should be offered to the participants. The transcript should show the date of the interview and the names of the participants, and should be filed with the other documents which the report writer has collected. However, it must be said that, generally speaking, written evidence for report writers should be used more often than spoken evidence.

Writing letters can also be a means of collecting information. The report writer could, for instance, use letters to inquire of suppliers about equipment and may, indeed, have to do so. Such letters and interviews with travellers and firms' representatives, may be used to supplement each other.

There are several points about the collection of material which the report writer should consider carefully. The first is that he should acquire what can be called a sense of the value of the material he collects as he collects it. That is to say, he should always keep in mind the main object of the report which he has to write. He should learn to regard every scrap of material he collects in the light of its relevance to the terms of reference and the finished report. He should not let himself be diverted so that he comes to think too much about, or waste his time on, matters which are not relevant. For as he collects his material, all sorts of information are likely to come his way, and he should be able to judge quickly which of it is important for his needs and which of it is not. For instance—to take a quite obvious example about air-conditioning: in the course of his inquiries he may learn some interesting, but not relevant, facts about clean air in hotels, theatres and the maternity wards of hospitals. But clearly, since the proposed research station is not an hotel or a theatre, and is not likely to contain a maternity ward, he need not bother to deal with this information in his report.

The second point is that it is easy to be sidetracked in the course of an interview, or sometimes during a longish correspondence. The report writer, when he considers what has been said at an interview, should always be careful to distinguish fact from opinion. For what a person says may be only the expression of a personal point of view, and a personal point of view is not necessarily to be taken at its face value. If, for instance, the report writer is pursuing his inquiries into air-conditioning plant, and is told by someone who is showing him a particular kind of air filter that such a kind of air filter is difficult to clean, he must find out exactly what 'difficult to clean' means. Is it only the opinion of his informant, who has found personally that cleaning that kind of air filter is troublesome, or is it a question of the wrong sort of air filter having been fitted in the first place, or what?

A third point which the report writer must consider is the best way for him to make notes. Each individual will have his own views on the matter. Some people make notes, during an interview perhaps, on pages of a small lose-leaf notebook, and then transfer what they have written to cards which can be indexed. Some people prefer to make their notes directly on to the cards. Other people are more haphazard, and make their notes on any scrap of paper which is lying about. It is best, on the whole, to have some intelligible system, which can easily be explained to, and understood by, somebody else—such as the writer's secretary or typist—so that there is no doubt about the note-taker's intentions. Direct notes, too, are more likely to be accurate than copied notes. It is certainly always risky to make a copy of a copy. Therefore, even if copies of notes are to be made, the original notes should never be thrown away, but always kept as a check, and any copies that are made should always be made from the original.

One final question about the collection of material is worth asking. How does the report writer know when he has collected all the material that he will need? This is a fine test of the report writer's judgement. All the time he is collecting his material, he should be thinking about its relevance to the terms of reference. If he has interpreted the terms of reference correctly, and if he has made an accurate assessment of the tasks that have to be done so that the terms of reference can be complied with accurately, then the question should answer itself. It is normally likely that the writer will collect more information than he needs for the final report, but if he is good at his job, and always keeps his eye on his objective, he will never collect useless information, but merely statements which have to be condensed or summarized.

3.4 Evaluation and Ordering

The evaluation and ordering of the material are tasks which can usually be done while the material is being collected. By evaluation we mean deciding on the value of the material collected for its place in the final report. And by ordering we mean deciding on what that place is. It is always advisable to have second thoughts about these aspects before the actual writing of the first draft is begun. Many questions can be asked. Is all the material really necessary? What is the right order in which to present the material in view of the terms of reference and the probable readership? Does some of the material need to be given greater weight than others? If so, which and why? Does the report writer over-estimate or under-estimate the importance of some of the material he has gathered? Has he come too close to some of it, so that he cannot see the wood for the trees? Does he understand it so well that he may not appreciate the difficulties with it of those who have not studied it so deeply?

Such questions as these should always be asked and answered.

Let us now suppose that the report writer has collected the following information in response to the terms of reference given on page 25.

1. *Proposed new research station to be built on the Wilmorton site*
The building is to comprise three main parts—(1) administration wing, with offices, library, canteen, kitchen, first-aid room, (2) materials testing wing—workshop, welding shop, engine room (escaping steam, diesel oil fumes), and machines lab., (3) electronics laboratories wing—transistor and resistor research—perhaps new transducer materials in future—tests for electronics, computers, telecommunications materials for manufacturers all over the world. Stupid site to choose. Very bad polluted air all over the district. Should have chosen top of Mont Blanc.

2. *Table A: Dust content of air (England and Wales)*

Place	Average concentration mg/m³	Average grain size μm
Country		
dry weather	0·15	6·3
wet weather	0·05	1·3
Small towns in rural areas	0·4	15·6
Large industrial conurbations	4·0	500·0
Immediate environment of works using coal or oil fuel	12000·0	950·0

3. *General notes on air pollution*

There are three kinds of polluted air which are likely to be encountered in, and in the regions of, the industrial cities of the U.K. Sometimes, and most frequently, these kinds are found to be co-existing. Dust is the prime cause of most pollution. Dust, which is airborne, consists of particles of dispersed solids which can be graded as coarse, medium or fine. This dust comprises both organic and inorganic matter. Organic dust can be pollen, seeds, small insects, bacteria and micro-organisms. Sometimes this kind of dust becomes attracted to inorganic dust. Inorganic dust is normally soot, ash, sand, dry clay, dry earth, mineral substances, and even in the immediate environment of foundries and blast furnaces small particles of metals. The amount of dust in the atmosphere of a particular environment varies according to the weather conditions, the humidity of the air, seasonal changes, etc. Particles of dust, ranging in diameters from 1000 or more to less than 0·1 μm are likely to fall on the site area. During the winter months, this dust will chiefly comprise soot and ash, since the site is on the south-east side of the City, but during the summer months may also comprise seeds and pollen and some insect life, especially in anticyclonic weather conditions which may be experienced in June or July and early August.

Also in polluted air can be found what are called aerosols. These are molecules of solids or liquids which emanate from a variety of sources, the chief being various industrial processes (e.g. chemical plants, especially those producing plastic substances, breweries, etc.). Inside some buildings (e.g. theatres, cinemas, department stores, dance halls, colleges, schools, etc.) where large concentrations of human beings could be found at fixed times, minute quantities of aerosols may arise from tobacco smoke, the chewing of sweets, con-

fections, chewing gum, and from human perspiration. Similarly
minute quantities of aerosols also arise from sewage, abattoirs,
broilers, gas works, oil refineries, and, in rural areas, from farm
animals and decaying vegetable matter. They also occur in kitchens
and other places where food is cooked or prepared by heating.
Unlike dust, aerosols do not fall through the atmosphere towards
the surface of the earth, but their behaviour is comparable to
molecules of gas and they obey the laws of Brownian motion.
However, in or near the more intensively industrialized centres they
tend to be absorbed by the comparatively large dust particles and
thus to fall towards the earth when so absorbed. The concentration
of aerosols in the air of both rural and industrialized urban areas is,
however, very small, though it varies according to location and
prevailing wind. In Birmingham and Stoke-on-Trent, for instance,
it is about 3% by weight, but in Liverpool it is only approx. 2%
on account of the latter's marine atmosphere and prevailing wind.

Also to be found in polluted air are gases in very small quantities.
These are chiefly carbon monoxide from the combustion of coal and
petroleum products, and sulphur dioxide which also comes from the
combustion of coal and petroleum products. The quantities of these
gases likely to be experienced on the site, however, are negligible
and may safely be ignored.

4. *Air intakes*
Problem of location of air intakes. Should not face streets. High ones
best, on account of swirling dust. Always intervene building between
intaken air and main sources of pollution, i.e. south or east side of
research station. East side would mean over car park and service
road to kitchen and main materials testing lab. Architect suggests
over electronics labs wing at least forty feet from ground level. Also
different intake and outlet on south side of materials testing wing.

5. *Table B: Dust concentration on site (mean for 12 weeks Feb 3 to Apl 25 19—)*

Weather	Mean concentration mg/m³	Average grain diameter μm	Largest grain diameter μm
dry	0·65	21	11000
wet	0·35	16	900

These tests were made by Mr A. B. C—— of the City's Smoke-
abatement Department. Both Martius gravimetric and Konimeter

air-intake devices were used. Chemical analysis of the dust collected
by the Konimeter air-intake device showed that the dust chiefly
consisted of soot and ash, with a comparatively high, though still
negligible, proportion of sulphur dioxide.

6. *Air-conditioning plant*

Three main types—air washers, air filters and electrostatic precipitators.

Air washers, because of their low efficiency, would be quite unsuitable.

Air filters can be grills, screens, gauzes, etc., located at point of
intake. Prevent dust, leaves, insects, paper, and odd rubbish finding
ingress into the system. They can also be wet or dry filters installed
in the system behind the grill or screen at intake point or at intervals
along the air ducts.

Wet or adhesive filters—mostly made of oil-wetted metal fibres,
laminates of steel wool, fibreglass, etc. Low-viscosity mineral oil
is used as recommended by manufacturers. They can be obtained
either as fixed panels or as continuous strips moving through a bath
of oil and powered off the same motor that operates the fans in the
air ducts.

Dry filters—obtainable as screen panels—made of various fibrous
materials—fibreglass, metal wool, electrostatic plastic fibres. Also
as laminated screens with materials of different densities, so that
coarse dust is separated first, less coarse dust next, and so on.

N.B.—just noted: *Factory Production*, Jan 19—, page 87, article
on new filter medium—kind of carbon-fibre or plastic high polymer?
—for commercial reasons actual material not stated. Screens of
standard sizes, as well as laminated screens. Seem reasonable.

Electrostatic filters or precipitators—air carrying dust is passed
through baffles of electrically charged metal coated with oil, so that
dust is collected on these baffles whose ionized field attracts it. Needs
high voltage. Flashovers may occur. Maintenance troublesome.
Separation not high at low voltage. Power consumption—say 5 W
per 1000 cubic yards per hour throughput. Expensive.

All that, then, could be some of the material that might be
found in the files of a man who has to write a report on this
matter of air pollution likely to be met with on the particular
site mentioned in the terms of reference, and on the kinds of
air-conditioning equipment likely to be needed. He may, of
course, have collected much more, and a great deal will be
carried in his memory. Also on his desk may be articles from

periodicals, books he may have borrowed from the library, as well as plans, maps, graphs, charts, and so on.

Having collected the material, the writer has to ask himself what he can make of it. And before he can answer that question, he must look again at the terms of reference. In the light of the terms of reference given on page 25, the information given in item 1 is clearly of some importance. But the information in item 2 is irrelevant and could be left out. So could the information given in item 4—air intakes will become a matter for the architects and the ventilating engineers who install the equipment at a much later date. Much of the badly written 'General Notes on Air Pollution' may be interesting background information to some people, including perhaps the report writer himself, but it is only likely to waste the time of potential readers of the report. The writer of this book thinks that it is a long, rambling account of air pollution written in bad English, and although some of the information may be of some importance somewhere, most of it is time-wasting and off the point: the second paragraph, for instance, is full of unwanted material. What is given in item 5 is obviously useful, but not by itself, for it has to be related to the needs of the proposed buildings. It has therefore to be connected in some way with the information that is provided in items 1 and 6. For the material which we have read makes no suggestions about what sort of air-conditioning equipment is likely to be needed. We should want to know, for instance, whether all the rooms in the proposed buildings need to have air of the same purity. Do the corridors and staircases in the administration wing, for instance, need air of the same purity as the laboratories in the electronics laboratories wing? Does the air in the lift shafts have to be as cleanly filtered as the air in, say, rooms used for assembling transistors or rooms which may house delicate scientific instruments? Or how is the escaping steam and diesel fumes from the engine room going to affect the atmosphere outside the building? All that item 6 states, very sketchily, is what kinds of air-conditioning equipment there are. And nowhere does the material say how these kinds are to be related to the needs of the research station.

Nevertheless, it is no bad thing for the report writer to move in and about, through and round, the subject-matter of his report in this way. For, provided he does not waste too much time, it does give him a good insight into what he is talking about. And also it does enable him to master his subject, so that he can speak, or appear to be speaking, with the voice of authority. Even so, the dangers are obvious. It is all too easy to get bogged down in a mass of useless information, and to flounder about not knowing in which direction to go next. The report writer must always keep in mind what the purpose of his particular report is, so that he can see his way clearly through all the material he collects.

3.5 Drafting, Writing and Revising

Drafting the report is setting out some plan for the actual composition of it, for the writer must know what the report is to say, how it is to say it, and what is the distribution of the main contents among the different parts. The writing, of course, is simply the job of getting on with writing down what has to be written—but this is, perhaps, for many people, the most difficult job of all. And the revision is the final checking to see that the job is well done.

These three jobs should be done in as much privacy as possible, and, if it can be arranged, away from the intrusions of other work, of telephone calls, or of visitors who may interrupt. To produce good writing most people need fairly long quiet periods in which they can get on with their work undisturbed, and in which they can concentrate on what they are doing without having to bother with anything else. In a busy factory, or in offices where people are constantly coming and going, where a telephone may ring at any time, and where a man may be suddenly called away to attend to something different from what he has set his mind on, it is not always easy to find a private haven of quiet. But the effort should be made.

The first job of drafting is to find some logical ordering of the material which shall give what we shall call *cohesion* to the report. This cohesion, which we shall talk about later, is the systematic arranging of all that the report has to say so that it can become an efficient signal to convey the message. And the message is simply the information that the report is called upon to present in relation to the terms of reference.

Many report writers in industry and research seem to think of their reports in terms of the kind of essays which they had to write at school. Therefore, without bothering too much during the drafting stage about the *form* of the final report, they simply give a chronological account of their investigations and findings. They might produce something like this:

AIR POLLUTION AND AIR-CONDITIONING REQUIREMENTS FOR NEW
RESEARCH STATION BUILDINGS AT WILMORTON

Ref: XYZ/123/45   *26 May 19—*

Three kinds of air pollution are likely to be experienced on the site and in the region of the site of the proposed new research station buildings at Wilmorton. These are dust, aerosols and gases. The air-borne dust in that area consists of dispersed solids in the atmosphere which can be graded as coarse, medium or fine. Particles of these ranging from upwards of 1000 to less than 0·1 μm in diameter are likely to fall on the site area. During the winter period the dust will chiefly comprise soot and ash since the site is on the south-east side of the City of ——, while during the summer months the dust will in addition comprise seeds and pollen, especially in anti-cyclonic weather conditions. Aerosols are molecules of solids or liquids very thinly distributed in the atmosphere, and in or near industrial regions tend to be absorbed by large dust particles, therefore constituting a very small part of the total atmospheric impurity, with a mean concentration of about 3% by weight of the total dust particles. Small quantities of carbon monoxide and sulphur dioxide gases, especially the latter, may also be found on the site area.

Tests were carried out by Mr A. B. C——, Assistant to the Smoke-abatement Officer of the City of ——, to determine the dust content of the air on the site, and extended over a period of twelve (12) weeks from February 3rd to April 25th inclusive. During dry weather conditions the mean concentration of dust in the atmosphere was found to be 0·65 milligrams per cubic metre, the average grain diameter was 21·0 μm, the largest being 11,000 μm. During wet weather conditions these findings were found to have fallen to 0·35 milligrams per cubic metre, and 16·0 and 900 μm respectively. Both a Martius gravimentric apparatus and a Konimeter air-intake apparatus were utilized. Chemical analysis of the dust gathered by the Konimeter showed that the dust comprised chiefly soot and ash with a negligible proportion of sulphur dioxide. The amount of organic matter in the dust was also found to be negligible, though Mr A. B. C—— reported that in the summer months this proportion would be slightly increased due to seeds, pollen and insects.

Air-conditioning equipment can be divided into three main categories: air washers, air filters, and electronic precipitators. With air washers the polluted air is brought into contact with moving water, either continuously fresh or cleaned and recirculated. These are, however, of low separation efficiency, as the coarse dust only is removed, while in urban atmospheres, where oily particles may exist, these are not removed at all, and damage to sophisticated electronic equipment may therefore result. They are therefore not recommended. Air filters can be divided into two sorts, adhesive filters and dry filters. Adhesive filters mostly have oil-wetted metal or plastic fibres. Dry filters have various kinds of fibre fabrics fitted in panels which can easily be removed for cleaning or replacement. Both these kinds have a separation efficiency of 90% plus, and the latter are the kind in most common use today. Electronic precipitators, on account of the fact that they are expensive to maintain, are not recommended, although the separation efficiency is high.

In view of the fact that the proposed new research station buildings are deployed in three wings (*vide* sketch-map attached), and that the wings have differing functions, there will be two degrees of air purity required. In the main administration wing and the materials testing wing (except for the Laboratories A and B on the top floor), only a medium to a high degree of air purity will be required, and in the engine room of this latter wing no air-conditioning strictly speaking will be required at all, while in the electronics laboratories wing a consistently high to very high degree of air purity will be constantly required twenty-four hours of the day. It will therefore be necessary to condition the air of each wing by means of three different sets of plant, and it will be necessary to have plant which can deal with 25,000 cubic yards of air per hour, this being 6000 for the administration wing, 9000 for the materials testing wing and 10,000 for the electronics laboratories wing. It is recommended that the architect should allow for a so-called duo-duct system capable of maintaining this load, and that grade S, or special suspended-particle filters (which have a separation efficiency of nearly 100% down to a particle size of $0 \cdot 3$ μm), of the panel type be fitted in the electronics laboratories wing, and filters of grades B and C, according to requirements, elsewhere.

(Signed) C.D.E.

Many adverse criticisms can be made of this report. The first is that it is difficult for the reader to find his way about in it. The second is that it contains material which is not wanted. The third is that the English is poor.

Few people, as we have said, read reports for fun or
ment in their leisure time. Reading reports for thos
who have to read them is a duty, and it is a duty wh
like to see dispatched easily, quickly and efficiently. Th ҏoint
is that the reader of a report has a job of work to do; he wants
background information so that he can know how to take
action. Moreover, as we have also said, not all readers will
want to read a report for the same reasons.

The writer of the report given above has not taken his readers
into account. Nor has he clearly interpreted his terms of
reference. The first paragraph contains information which is
not wanted, and so does the third. It is easy to see that the
writer has collected more material than the report needs; and
while there can be no objection to this in principle, there can
be an objection to his not having selected reasonably from the
total material those parts which meet the terms of reference.

Both of these criticisms show that the writer has not seriously
considered the problem of *form*. We said in Chapter One that
the form of a report is a typical arrangement of parts which
make it characteristically a report, and not something else; and
in Chapter Two we suggested that the concept of form was a
very important one in acts of communication—indeed, that
acts of communication were nothing more than the transmission
and recognition of forms.

The writer of a report should therefore pay special attention
to this idea of form, and consider it as probably the most important aspect of what he has to say. If he is to consider his
readers, his first task, then, in the job of drafting, is to think
carefully about the form or shape of the lay-out and the
presentation. For instance, the writer of the report given above
might have blocked out on a sheet of paper the main headings
and sub-headings for parts of his subject-matter. The result
could have been something like this:

1. TITLE, with reference number	This is a brief factual statement, in as few words as possible, of the subject-matter. As part of the information-control of the firm or organization, the report will be filed, its title and reference number will be used for this purpose.

2. DATE

D

3. AIM

A statement of the terms of reference might come here, or at least a statement of the writer's purpose in producing the report. For, indeed, reports are written with a purpose in mind, and readers, therefore, want to know why they have to read them. Some readers may have several reports to read, and may want to be reminded of what reports have been called for, so if a statement of the aim is written near the beginning, a reader can see at a glance what the report is about, and he can thus be helped to concentrate his mind on its subject.

4. SUMMARY

A short précis of the whole report is given here, near the beginning, so that readers may have a general idea of what it is all about and what the main conclusions are. Those readers who do not want, or have not time, to read the whole document, may thus know which part or parts might interest them.

5. MAIN DISCUSSION

This is the real body of the report, and may have several parts. In the example we are considering here, the writer might have gone on, blocking out his sub-headings as follows, if he was convinced they were all needed:

(5.1) *Kinds of air pollution*
    (a) dust
    (b) aerosols
    (c) gases
(5.2) *Pollution of local air*
    (a) procedures for testing
    (b) results of tests
(5.3) *Air-conditioning equipment*
    (a) air washers
    (b) electrostatic precipitators
    (c) air filters
(5.4) *Needs of research station buildings*
    (a) short description of research station
    (b) administration wing
    (c) materials testing wing
    (d) electronics laboratories wing

6. CONCLUSIONS   A report, of course, must lead somewhere, and where it leads is to the conclusions that the writer has come to as a result of his inquiries. These conclusions may be merely a statement of some facts, for which the main discussion of the report has provided the whys and wherefores. Or the conclusions may be recommendations, if these are what the terms of reference asked for. If the writer is asked to make recommendations, they will arise naturally from the main discussion, which will give the reasons that led him to make them.

The advantage of organizing the lay-out of the report in some such way as this is that it helps both writer and reader. It helps the writer to have, first, a clear idea of what he is doing, for it should keep the purpose of the report firmly in his mind. Second, it can help him to organize his material in some objective and understandable manner. If the writer of the report given above had organized in this way from the start, he might have avoided the unnecessary paragraphs. For, third, this method can help the writer to form an appreciation of the relative value of the different sections of the material which he has collected; he will see it all spread out, as it were, on a map in front of him; he knows which bits go where, which bits are more important than the others, and which bits can be left out altogether.

Obviously, the headings and sub-headings of the various sections of the report will be carried through from the first drafting stage to the final product. In the finished report each heading or sub-heading will appear numbered and typed or written on a separate line. In this way the finished report will present a neat and workmanlike appearance to its readers. And what is more, the readers will be able easily to find their way about. The summary near the beginning will give the readers an opportunity to find out quickly what the whole report says, and then, if some of them do not want to read all of it, they can easily find those sections which they want to read, and either just glance at the others or ignore them.

It is important to note that this summary, although it comes at or near the beginning, should actually be written last. That is, in the final writing of the report, the writer should start with the main discussion—perhaps with each part on a separate sheet of paper, if he thinks that is a good idea—and build up the sections of the main discussion bit by bit, so that he comes logically to the conclusion and, if they are asked for, his recommendations. He will then have to go back, read through what he has thus far produced, and write the summary which can then be inserted in its place in the final draft of the report.

In Chapter Two we suggested that a report was a communication channel, that is, a physical device which organizes and controls a number of signals. Such signals are, first, the kinds of main headings we have just looked at—Title, Date, Aim, Summary, etc.—and then, second, the sentences that are written under them, as well as, third, any tables of statistics, graphs, diagrams, and so on, which may also form part of the report. This idea suggests that a report is an integrated structure of signals which make up a system. And a system is a whole composed of parts which articulate together. Each signal should convey a message to the reader. But where there are a number of signals, which convey associated messages, such signals have to be arranged and organized. The method of organization which we have suggested here displays the signals that make up the report, and it does so in such a way that at every point the reader should know what sort of message the signal is supposed to convey, and how the particular signal is connected with those associated with it, and which these connected signals are.

If a report is a systematic structure of displayed signals, there can be several ways of forming such a structure. Some books on report writing, especially American ones, often go to great lengths in explaining what these several ways are or can be imagined to be. But since, as we have already said, a report is always an individual act of communication, and no two reports are likely to arise in the same circumstances, to try to fit the art of report writing into a kind of strait-jacket is largely a waste of time. And in any case, all of the various ways are actually variations on the same theme. All of them are versions of some such general idea as this:

1. Title
2. Aim
3. Summary
4. Main discussion
5. Conclusions

Of course, the divisions of any report within this outline or framework will depend upon a number of different considerations, all of which will arise out of the nature of the report and its purpose. In some cases, if the report is a very short one, there may be no need for a summary, since the main discussion could be read so quickly that it could be regarded as a summary in itself. But this would apply only if the report were a very short one indeed—say, one of just half a dozen sentences or so. On the other hand, if the report were a very long one—say, anything upwards of ten to fifteen closely-typed pages—it might not be a bad idea to supply a table of contents; this would then immediately follow the title (which would have a page all to itself), and would include, of course, the page numbers on which the terms of reference and the summary or abstract could be found. At the same time, the main divisions of the main discussion, with their numbered headings and page numbers, would also be included.

We also said that the report given on page 41 could be criticized for its bad English. Later, we shall look into the matter of the use of English in some detail, and the reader may care to look again through the report in the light of what he will read hereafter. What we think is bad in the use of English in the report is the presence of clichés—'likely to be experienced', 'weather conditions', 'on account of the fact that'. We also object to the lack of cohesion in some of the sentences—for example, in the next to the last sentence of the first paragraph. Nor do we like the confused way in which some of the information is presented—what is given in the second and third sentences of the second paragraph could have been better displayed by means of a table. And we do not like the dull, turgid, arid pedestrianism of the whole.

3.6 The Fair Copy

In the actual writing and revision of the report, the writer should aim to be fresh, interesting and informative. He should see to it that the parts of the report are arranged in such a way that the whole document is attractive to look at, so that the reader is not put off by its appearance right at the beginning.

The *title* should normally (unless the report is a very short one indeed) be given a page to itself. It should appear on the upper half of the page and should be distinctive, so that it can be seen at a glance. A potential reader, taking the document out of a folder or his briefcase, wants to see immediately what he is getting, and not go grubbing among his papers to discover what he wants. The wording of the title should be plain and unambiguous, and should include, if possible, the key word or key words of the terms of reference. Sometimes, also on the title page, will appear the name of the writer, the name of the department or section of the organization or firm in which the report originated, the reference number and the date.

The statement of the *aim* of the report should also closely follow the wording of the terms of reference, and often need be nothing more than a repetition of those terms. The writer will have to use his own judgement about this. Sometimes the terms of reference may be very long, and the report writer need only supply a précis. But such a précis does not always have to resemble the kind of précis he wrote at school—it need not be 'in his own words'. What is wanted is a short, clear statement of why the report came into existence.

The *summary* or abstract can be a separable part of the report. Its purpose is to state the main facts of all the report and its conclusions, so that someone can find out in a few moments what the report is all about without having to read it all. Sometimes summaries or abstracts are circulated separately with just this end in view, and then people who want more detailed information about the whys and wherefores of the whole subject-matter can call for copies of the entire report. The summary should state the main facts and conclusions, but should omit the discussion and comment that appear in the main body of the report.

It is in the writing of the *main discussion* that the real test of the report writer's ability appears. The first essential is for the writer to have a clear idea of what he is going to say and why he is going to say it. For this reason the main headings and sub-headings of the discussion must be thought out carefully, and the writer should remember that first thoughts are not necessarily the best thoughts.

If the report is going to be a very long one, the body of the report may need an introduction. This is a paragraph or section which should not be vague, but which should introduce the subject-matter and be relevant to it. This introductory part could, for instance, provide background information which is necessary for a proper understanding of what follows—say, a short statement of the events leading up to the problem which the report is intended to elucidate. Or it could describe briefly the way in which the writer intends to deal with his subject—say, the point of view from which it is presented, especially if this point of view is an unusual one, or if, during his preliminary inquiries, the writer has come across something unexpected or unforeseen. It might define the writer's technical terms. Or it might state the nature of the problem to be solved by the facts which he has discovered during his investigations. Or it might describe the writer's intended procedures in presenting the report—again, especially so if these are in some way un-usual or unexpected by the reader. It might happen, now and then, that the terms of reference are too wide or too narrow, or that those who frame the terms of reference are not com-pletely aware of all the facts, or have failed to grasp some significant point. If this is so, the writer will have to explain the case in his introduction to the body of the report. But the writer should convince himself of the necessity for such an introductory paragraph or section before it finds its way into the final report. He should try to put himself in the place of his readers and ask if it is helpful to them. If he cannot convince himself that it would be helpful, he should not bother with it.

While he is composing the main discussion, the writer should always be aware of what he is doing, paragraph by paragraph, sentence by sentence. He should be able to give adequate answers to such questions as, 'Why are there three paragraphs under that sub-heading—why not two or four?', or 'Why do these paragraphs appear in that particular order and not some other—why isn't the first put second and the second third?', or 'Why has this paragraph five sentences in it, and why are they in it in that order?' Questions like these are not silly, for if the writer can give sensible and intelligible answers to them, then such answers show that he understands his job.

The point is that a report, considered as an integrated structure of signals which make up a system, is also a logical presentation of ideas—or it should be. And ideas can only be presented in sentences and paragraphs or in substitutes for sentences and paragraphs in tables, diagrams and drawings. As we shall later see in some detail, every time a report writer presents an idea by means of sentences in paragraphs he is doing one of four things. He is giving a narration. Or he is giving a description. Or he is giving an explanation. Or he is presenting an argument. To put the matter another way: he is answering the question, 'What happens?'; or he is answering the question, 'What is it like?'; or he is answering the question, 'How?'; or he is answering the question, 'Why?'.

At every stage during the composition of the report, the writing will be fitting a portion of the structure into its place. His job is to know what its place is and why.

The *conclusion* of a report may simply be a statement of the results of the writer's investigations, and if it is, these should follow naturally from the main discussion. Normally, the writer should not come to his task with his mind already made up. Therefore he should not rig his investigations or arrange the main discussion to fit any preconceived ideas of a conclusion he may have come to. The facts should be allowed to speak for themselves, and if they are set out in the logically correct way should also inevitably lead to the conclusion. In other words, the conclusion should be a statement of the logical deductions or inferences that can be made from the facts presented in the main body of the report.

The statements given in the conclusion can be of two kinds. They can simply give the results of the writer's inquiries without any further comment, or they can, in addition to these, give the writer's recommendations about what he thinks ought to be done. The terms of reference will help here. They may just ask for conclusions, or they may ask for recommendations as well. If recommendations are wanted, they should be stated in a separate section or paragraph, or set out as a list with each recommendation numbered. There should be good reasons for the recommendations, which may have to be discussed or thought about by those who will eventually read the report, and on which further action may be taken. Therefore the recommendations should come naturally and logically from the conclusions, and why they come naturally and logically should be obvious to the readers.

Lastly, it should be remembered that, after the report has been written, revised and checked by the writer, it will have to be typed, and may have to be duplicated or photographically copied for circulation to its readers, and may even have to be printed. The writer should therefore give careful instructions to his typist about how the typing should be done. First of all, the typist should be in no doubt about what she has to type. All unusual words, all scientific and technical terms, numerals and mathematical symbols should be clearly legible, and therefore easily reproduced by someone who may not understand them. Spelling and usages should be consistent. All material should be correctly arranged in sequence, and each page of the writer's manuscript should be clearly numbered. The typist should have no doubts about the place in the report of additional matter—the author's second thoughts, corrections, and such items as tables, graphs, diagrams, and so on. Secondly, the finished copy should have a clean and fresh appearance to make it look attractive to the reader. Preferably double spacing should be used by the typist for the main prose of the report. There should be good margins on either side—from fifteen to twenty spaces on the left and at least ten spaces on the right. (The author of this book has been to many meetings at which reports have been received and discussed, and has always cursed those copies in which there was not enough room to make pencilled notes in the margins.) Headings and subheadings should be clearly displayed and distinguished, and the numbers of headings, sections and paragraphs should be so managed that they can be quickly found and read. Finally, the report writer should encourage his typist to consult him always about any difficulties, no matter how trivial they may seem, of lay-out and minor points which may arise during the typing. If he is going to produce a good job, he must never expect to be able to give his manuscript to her and hope that she will be able to get on without his help.

Chapter four:
The Use of English

4.1 Why English is Important

Upon the use of English depends the quality of the thought conveyed, the clarity of the ideas that are to be expressed, and the understanding by the reader of what the writer is talking about.

There is no doubt that a great deal of bad, and often very bad, English is used every day by scientists and technologists, and most of it, surprisingly, seems to be due to an absence of clear thinking. The writers are, perhaps, fully acquainted with their specialist skills and knowledge, but when they come to write about what they are supposed to be experts on, they seem to think that the most slapdash way of expressing their ideas is permissible and that anything will do. This is a grave mistake, because bad habits can easily spread. The English language is a tool, a piece of valuable and delicate equipment, absolutely necessary if communication is to take place at all. Those people who keep the apparatus and equipment in their laboratories and workshops in first-class working order, and who would not for a moment tolerate dirty machines, untidy work benches, or tools which had been allowed to deteriorate, seem unable to devote the same kind of care and consideration to the English language. The result is that the tool of language becomes clogged and unworkable, and communication is therefore hindered by bad habits of thought, the rust and corrosion of misuse, and the damage of careless handling.

Here is a typical example taken at random from a technical report:

> The purpose of the storage tank is to uncouple the rates of flow upstream and downstream; it does this in such a way that a change in one flow produces a change in the other which is smaller in magnitude than it would otherwise have been, or which occurs at a different time.

The point is, presumably, that the purpose of the storage tank is to store some liquid (oil in this case) so that a supply will always be available, but the rate of flow into the tank is not the same as that from it, so the tank is fitted with some device which equalizes the difference by slowing down or stopping the inward flow. But how can anything 'uncouple' two different rates of flowing of a liquid? And what does the pronoun *it* after the semi-colon refer to—the purpose of the tank or the tank itself? Normal understanding of English would show that it refers to the noun *purpose*, but this makes nonsense of the part of the extract that begins with the word *it* after the semi-colon, since it is the tank itself and not its purpose 'does this in such a way'. And why does the author use the unnecessary verbiage of *smaller in magnitude*, when one can save time, ink, paper and money, as well as avoid irritating the sensitive reader, by simply saying 'smaller'?

Here is another example:

> A number of schemes already exist which facilitate the training of young engineers abroad. Some of these are formally organized by engineering companies whilst, at the other end of the spectrum, certain organizations arrange travel and the onus is upon the individual to make his own arrangements for gaining some educational benefit.

What the author means, one imagines, is this: 'Many British firms allow young engineers to be trained abroad; some organize their schemes formally, others pay only the trainee's expenses and leave him to arrange his own training.' This uses twenty-nine words to say what the extract says in fifty-two. Even so, since the original is not very clear, it is difficult to know what the author really meant. Such an expression as *a number of schemes already exist* is both beating about the bush—not getting directly to the subject—and vague; what is to be understood by the word *number*—is it many, or some, or just a few? And why use the unnecessary and ambiguous verbiage of *which facilitate the training of young engineers abroad*? Presumably the training takes place abroad—but it is for young engineers in this country who are sent abroad to receive it, not the young engineers already there. The word facilitate means 'to make easy'; and one imagines that it is not the training itself which is facilitated, but the opportunities to receive it. The second sentence of the extract is unnecessarily long. What does the metaphor in *at the other end of the spectrum* contribute to the reader's understanding? A spectrum is an image formed by radiation in which parts are arranged according to their wavelengths. Does the author mean that different kinds or sizes of firms can be likened to such an image? If he does, what is the point of his doing so? And why does the author think it necessary to use the long-winded expression *the onus is upon the individual to make his own arrangements for gaining some educational benefit*? The point is that the more nouns, or names of things, one brings into a sentence, the more one gives the reader to think about; give him too much to think about all at once, and one confuses him. In the second sentence of the extract the author uses nine nouns; in the corresponding part of our rewriting we have used three. Moreover, is the 'gaining of some educational benefit' the same sort of thing as 'receiving training'? Or is the author merely trying to find ways of trying to show off with words by not repeating himself?

Here is another example:

Advantages of the new method of membrane panel construction include a minimum of weld penetration with high frequency welding, and this has enabled thinner tubes to be utilized, so enabling the membrane wall design to be extended to the medium- and low-pressure boiler ranges. Another advantage is that the new type of joint design calls only for structural welds instead of pressure part welds in the original design.

This is a whole paragraph. Clearly, when the reader sees the first word *advantages*, he is led to believe that the advantages of the new method is the topic of the paragraph. But how many advantages are there? Surely that is a question which someone reading a report on this new method is entitled to have

answered; he might, in fact, be reading the report just to discover that information. But we are told what the advantages
'include', as if the advantages comprised something in them
other than themselves; and then in the second sentence of the
paragraph we are introduced to 'another advantage' as a kind
of afterthought. Presumably there are three advantages. If so,
a good way of starting the paragraph would be to say just that—
'This method has three advantages.' At least, one imagines
there are three. But the expression *a minimum of weld penetration
with high frequency welding* is not very clear. Does it mean that
one advantage is a minimum of weld penetration when high-
frequency welding is used, or that the minimum is one advantage and high-frequency welding is another? One imagines
that the author means the former, since the word *this* presumably refers to one advantage and not two, but should one
have to read further on to discover the meaning of what you
are reading now? The paragraph could say, then, that one
advantage is this minimum of weld penetration when high-
frequency welding is used, that the second is a result of this,
because 'thinner' tubes can be used to make it possible extend
the membrane-wall design to the use of medium- and low-
pressure boilers, and that the third advantage is that this new
type of design for the joints needs only structural welds and
not pressure part-welds. But what are thinner tubes—those of
smaller bore or those with thinner walls? Does not the construction of the second part of the first sentence, with its 'enabled'
and 'so enabling', confuse the reader? Why use the word *utilized* when *used* would do? And why use two words *calls for* when
the one word *needs* is enough?

Some readers might object that this kind of criticism of bad
English is petty and niggling, and that even if, looked at from
the point of view of one who wants high literary quality in all
writing, these extracts may be bad, nevertheless most people
who are likely to read them would know what they mean. Such
an objection misses the point. What is condemned in the kinds
of bad writing just exemplified is the lack of clear thought
behind them, the attitude of mind which suggests that communication in language is not really important, and the influence which such writing can have on the language as a whole.

One would think that when a writer is dealing with scientific and technical matters, clear thinking should be of prime importance, for if science and technology cannot be accurate, what can? Yet when a writer, speaking of the help which computers can give to a firm's methods of distributing its products, says, 'Distribution is the meat in the sandwich between production and sales', he shows that he is not thinking clearly at all, and certainly not accurately. How can there be a sandwich between production and sales? To say that there can be one is simply nonsense, and although surrealism may be acceptable in imaginative literature, it has no place at all in technical writing. If the writer of that sentence wants to suggest that a firm's methods of production, distribution and selling are like a sandwich, then he is just being silly—the metaphor means nothing, for a sandwich normally consists of two kinds of the same thing with something else between them, and production and selling are quite different sorts of activities. Or if the writer wants to suggest that distribution is very important, and should be carefully considered by top management, then why not say so? His metaphor, mixed up and not properly thought out, and above all, inaccurate, cannot be helpful.

This careless attitude towards the use of English cannot clarify communication, for it suggests that, while what is talked about may be important, the way in which it is talked about is of no importance whatever. Moreover, it is very inefficient. Time, paper and ink, are daily frittered away in producing turgid nonsense which is of no use to anybody.

One hears—too often—the use of the expression 'failure of communications', and many books on the techniques of management in industry are written to show how this failure is the cause of delays and misunderstandings, bad human relations, lost production and inefficient working. If this is so, then a good place to start making improvements would be in the use of that essential tool of communication, the language itself. Nobody uses language naturally; everybody has to learn how to use it, and in the complicated kind of world in which we live there are many complicated uses to which we have to put the language. But learning needs effort; and it seems that many people are willing to learn the scientific principles and facts of their specialist studies and their applications in industry, but are not willing to learn how to express themselves clearly.

The influence which bad English can have on the language as a whole is enormous. The use of bad English is like a cancerous growth, which, from quite small beginnings, can spread and eventually kill the body in which it lives. The point is that when some people read expressions like 'broad categories' in technical writing, they actually come to believe that broad categories can exist, and that the expression has some meaning. When they read some such expression as 'smaller in magnitude', they come to believe that it is good and proper to use the expression again and again. Bad habits are infections and multiply. A very large number of people who have to write technical reports are not professional writers, and so they put down on paper the technical jargon of their trades in a way which they think sounds effective. They have not learnt to understand the difference between spoken and written English, and they have not learnt that expressing oneself in writing is much more difficult than expressing oneself in casual conversation. Good expression in writing can come only from clear thinking, and clear thinking must be able to manage not only the individual sentences, but also their organization into paragraphs, and the paragraphs into a complete composition. As soon as some people take up a pen to write, clear thinking seems to desert them, and the organization of the whole of what they are trying to express seems to be too much for them.

4.2 Good English is Readable

Since all reports are likely to have readers, all reports should be readable.

This statement suggests an important question which should be pondered carefully by all people who have to compose documents which other people will have to read in the course of their work. The question is this: How is it possible for a reader to be able to understand a sentence which he has not seen before the moment of reading?

For this does happen. Every day we are all presented in books and periodicals with sentences which we have not come across before in our lives—and yet we are able to understand them immediately.

The answer to the question was hinted at in Chapter Two.

We said there that communication in language depended on five interrelated codes, and that one of these was a grammatical code. And a code, we said, was a prearranged set of signs. We also suggested that the number of signs in a code was finite— if it were not, human memory would not be able to cope with it. As things are, human memory cannot cope with all the signs of the code of words—no speaker or writer knows *all* the words in the English language; but then, speakers and writers do not have to know them all, since they know enough for their purposes, and occasionally learn new words as occasion serves. But sentences are more important; if he is to communicate at all, a speaker or writer must put words into sentences. The basis of the grammatical code of English is a small fixed number of sentence forms. In accordance with the rules or conventions of this code, speakers and writers, listeners and readers arrange words in agreed patterns to produce what are called sentences. There is a limited number of ways in which these sentence patterns can be made. In other words, sentence patterns are signs, and the users of the language are able to recognize them as such because of their *form*.

The users of the language—speakers and writers, listeners and readers—are able to do this because they have been learning how to do it since earliest childhood. The knowledge has therefore become largely unconscious. Normally, when we speak or write, we tend to think more about what we are saying than about the way we say it. But if we want a fuller understanding of what we are doing, especially what we are doing when we are writing, which is more difficult than speaking, then we have to bring this unconscious knowledge to the surface so that we can see it more clearly.

If we know what the small fixed number of sentence forms or patterns is, and what each is like, then we can understand what sort of sentence form or pattern we are making every time we write a sentence. In this manner, we can increase the *readability* of our sentences, because we can thus make them into the kinds of signs that are recognizable by readers.

There are five basic sentence patterns used in English, and sentences are constructed in accordance with them or with their code on three main principles. From three of these five basic patterns, four others can be derived, making nine patterns in all. In addition to these nine main patterns, there are, also derived from the five basic patterns, those kinds of sentences which are called questions and commands. Not all these kinds of sentence patterns occur with the same frequency; some are very much more popular than others, for the sentence patterns, of course, correspond to the kinds of things we want to say, and we find that we want to say some kinds of things more often than others.

The three principles which govern the making of sentence patterns in English can be stated as:

First: in the making of sentence patterns speakers and writers name what is spoken about and then state what the thing spoken about does, did or will do, or is.

Second: any sentence pattern consists of a small fixed number of parts which normally appear in a fixed and conventionally agreed order.

Third: each or any of the parts of this small fixed number can be expanded or modified without disturbance of the conventionally agreed order.

The first of these principles merely repeats what most of us learnt at school, namely, that sentences consist of a subject and a predicate, and this is the primary and most basic pattern on which all English sentences are constructed. However, there are five basic sentence patterns in all because there are five different kinds of predicate. The second principle states this in a general way, since the five predicates are constructed in five different arrangements according to the distribution of their parts. It is this arrangement or patterning which makes the sentences into signs, so that we can distinguish any one from any of the others by means of its form, which is a patterning of these parts. The third principle states how the vast variety of English sentences is derived from the basic patterning—the parts are extended or elaborated in various ways which can be comprehended under the name of modification.

The five basic sentence patterns and their derivatives have evolved in society as speakers and writers have used the language. These patterns represent the ways in which speakers and writers want to speak and write about what they have to say. That is,

E

people want to do different kinds of things with sentences, and
so have evolved different kinds of sentences to do them.

We can illustrate all this by considering five sentences taken
from technical reports. Each sentence provides an example of
one of the five basic patterns and is given with comments.

(1) The temperature of the metal rises as energy is absorbed.

Here, the basic ingredients that give the sentence its characteristic pattern are the words *temperature rises*. All the other eight
words in this ten-word sentence are modification of one kind or
another, saying the temperature of what and when this temperature rises. This first basic pattern therefore has two parts,
a subject and predicate, and the predicate consists of one part
only, a verb. There is, consequently, a very close connexion
between these two parts, for the kind of activity or behaviour
expressed by the verb does not extend beyond what is referred
to by the subject. The sentence form exists to express this idea,
that something does something without any relationship to anything else. The verb is subject-oriented, and is very often a verb
of motion.

(2) The remote-control actuator is mechanically self-locking.

The basic ingredients that give the sentence its characteristic
pattern here are the words *actuator is self-locking*. The pattern is
thus made of three parts, a subject and a predicate which consists of two parts. Again, the other three words *the, remote-control*
and *mechanically* are modification. This pattern is a very common one, for it is the basis of all definitions and all of a vast
number of sentences which are used to describe. It is a pattern
used for saying what things, ideas or concepts are and what
they are like, or what speakers and writers think of them as
being like. The reader should note the connexion between the
third part, *self-locking*, and the first part or subject, *actuator*. In
this particular case the quality or attribute of being self-locking
belongs intimately to the actuator, and the verb in the sentence,
is, declares this to be so. The verb is again subject-oriented.

However, sentences built on this pattern normally use only
a very small number of verbs, usually the verbs *to be, to seem* and
to become, along with, sometimes the verb *to appear* when it
means the same as *to seem*. These verbs belong to a very special

group, in that they are not, as it were, self-contained in the same way as the verbs used in the first basic pattern are. If some-one begins a sentence 'The actuator is/seems/becomes . . .', and then stops speaking, his listener naturally wants to know what the actuator is or seems to be or becomes. These verbs, there-fore, need something, as the grammar books say, 'to complete the sense'. This something is a complement, which is a word or group of words which state what class of things the thing named by the subject belongs to, or which state something as being a member of some class, or which state some quality or attribute. For example: 'Elizabeth is *queen*' (where *queen* names the class of human beings to which Elizabeth belongs); or 'The Queen is Elizabeth' (where *Elizabeth* denotes membership of the class of queens); or 'Elizabeth is royal' (where *royal* states a quality or attribute).

(3) This change of design increases the output to over 700 watts.

This sentence is given its characteristic pattern by the three words *change increases output*. The words, *this, of design, the,* and *to over 700 watts* make up different sorts of modification. Again, the pattern is made of three parts, a subject, and a predicate which has two parts. But there is here an important difference from the pattern of the second type, and this difference is indicated by the verb *increases*. This is a verb which is not subject-oriented. It denotes an activity or kind of behaviour which, so to speak, does not stay with the subject, but which passes on to something else. This something else, here exempli-fied by the word *output*, is a word which stands for something different from what the subject stands for. Sentences con-structed according to this pattern, therefore, bring together the ideas of two different things and relate them in some way by which an activity on the part of what is denoted by the first affects what is denoted by the second. This second part of the predicate which comes after the verb is called the object.

It is in sentences of this pattern, which are among the most common in the English language, that we can see how important the order of words is in English. In fact, we can only know which is subject and which is object in most cases from the sign which is the order. A sentence such as 'Harry hit George' means something very different from the sentence 'George hit

Harry', and it is only the order of the words that can tell the reader what the difference is.

(4) The layer of foil gives the cable that protection needed in wet weather.

This sentence receives its characteristic pattern from the four words *layer gives cable protection*. The words, *the, of foil, the, that* and *needed in wet weather*, are, once more, various kinds of modification. This time the pattern is made of four parts, a subject and a three-part predicate. And again, it is the verb which is the dominating influence in making the characteristic pattern. For it is impossible to think of the idea of giving (or associated ideas represented by such words as *bestow, donate, grant, assign, present, deliver, endow*, etc.) without thinking also of something given to somebody or something else. Sentences of this pattern, therefore, need to have in the predicate two parts which come after the verb, one part which names the receiver of what is given, and another which states what is given to the receiver. The first part of these two is called the indirect object and the second part the object.

(5) Reconstitution makes cold-rolling easier.

Here is a sentence that happened to turn up in its basic form without any kind of modification. This, too, is a pattern of four parts, a subject and a predicate with three parts. Sentences of this pattern are not common, but they do occur occasionally. Their characteristic is that they are like sentences of the third pattern with an additional part, another kind of complement, which is needed to complete the sense. For such a statement as 'Reconstitution makes cold-rolling' is clearly nonsensical, and the complement *easier*, in this example, is necessary to make the utterance comprehensible.

It will be seen that the verbs in sentence patterns (3), (4) and (5) are very different from those in patterns (1) and (2). Grammatically, the difference can be defined by saying that patterns (3), (4) and (5) have verbs which are followed by an object, and patterns (1) and (2) do not. Looked at from the point of view of meaning, or the use to which such patterns are put by speakers and writers, it can be said that sentences of patterns (1) and (2) are more likely to be subjective, and sentences of patterns (3), (4) and (5) are more likely to be objective. That is to say, sentences of patterns (1) and (2) are about what goes on in the minds of speakers and writers, while sentences of patterns (3), (4) and (5) are about what goes on in the world outside the mind. This may be a difficult point to grasp, but it is an important one. It may, perhaps, be elucidated by comparing two grammatical subjects of sentences, say, the words *The temperature* from the first sentence, and the words *The layer of foil* from the fourth. What the words *The temperature* refer to is a mental concept, that is, what is measured or shown by a thermometer, a man-made device which alters as a function of something else. On the other hand, *The layer of foil* is an expression which refers to some physical thing and not to a mental concept. In other words, sentences of patterns (1) and (2) represent ideas or concepts which men assert about and impose on the external world. This can be seen in the idea of definition, for millions of definitions that have been made are sentences of pattern (2). We can say, for instance, 'A watt is a unit of electrical power', or 'A watt is the work done per second when 1 ampere flows under a potential of 1 volt', or 'A watt is equal to 1/746 horse power'. That is, a watt is whatever men choose to say it is. In making definitions, people are just putting words together, and what is defined becomes what the words say.

Another property of sentences of patterns (3), (4) and (5), which makes them different from the first two, is that they can be expressed in the passive voice. That is, the sentence, 'This change of design increases the output to over 700 watts', can be expressed as 'The output is increased to over 700 watts by this change of design'. Or the sentence, 'The layer of foil gives the cable that protection needed in wet weather', can be turned into the passive voice in two ways—first, 'The cable is given that protection needed in wet weather by the layer of foil', and second, 'That protection needed in wet weather is given the cable by the layer of foil'. Or the sentence, 'Reconstitution makes cold-rolling easier', can be expressed in the passive voice as 'Cold-rolling is made easier by reconstitution'.

Thus we have added four more to the main sentence patterns, and given examples of all the sentence patterns in English except those of questions and commands.

The five basic patterns could be set out in a table, something like this:

	Subject	Predicate				
		Verb	Complement$_1$	Indirect object	Object	Complement$_2$
1	X	X				
2	X	X	X			
3	X	X			X	
4	X	X		X	X	
5	X	X			X	X

In scientific and technical literature, there is a tendency to use the passive voice forms of sentences more than in any other kind of writing. The intention is to give impersonality. Instead of saying, in the course of a report, 'I recorded the temperature every 30 minutes', or even, 'My lab-assistant recorded the temperature at 30 minute intervals', technical and scientific writers seem to prefer to say, 'The temperature was recorded at 30 minute intervals'.

There is a pseudo-objectivity in this usage. For it only pretends to be objective without actually being so. But it has become part of the accepted technical and scientific style, and one assumes that it has unfortunately come to stay.

However, the widespread use of the passive voice has the serious disadvantage of obscuring what is really being said. This is because, in practice, a true passive voice is not used, and the emasculated passive that does get used tends to make sentences which are not actually of pattern (2) look as if they were. Consider, for example, this sentence from a technical report:

All batches of metal were made in a coke-fired crucible furnace, using 50 to 60 lb charges of 100 per cent hematite.

The basic ingredients of this sentence would seem to be the three words *batches were made*, and all the rest is modification of one kind or another. These three words tend to make what looks like a subject-verb-complement pattern. But is this actually so? When we turned the active sentences given above into the passive, the subject of the active sentence always appeared in the passive version in a phrase beginning with the word *by*—'by this change of design', 'by the layer of foil', 'by reconstitution'. But the sentence given above is a passive one with its *by*-phrase missed out. After all, somebody must have made the batches of metal; they could not have made themselves. In this case, the basic ingredients of the sentence should be *batches were made by somebody*, which is the passive version of an active pattern (3) *somebody made the batches*. And if somebody did it, why not say so? If a man is responsible enough—or if other people judge him to be responsible enough—to be entrusted with the making of batches of metal and carry out experiments in a foundry, why should he be ashamed to admit it?

Also in this particular case, the passive leads to a confusion of thought. Presumably the active version of the sentence would read, 'I made all batches of metal in a coke-fired crucible furnace, using 50-lb to 60-lb charges of 100 per cent hematite'. And that sentence is all right, for there is no unrelated participle. That is, the participle *using* clearly relates to the pronoun *I*; and since it is possible to say intelligibly, 'I am using . . .', there is no confusion of thought. But in the passive version of the original, the sentence seems to say that all batches of metal were using 50-lb to 60-lb charges, and that is absurd, because at that stage the batches of metal did not exist—how could they use anything before they were made?

We said earlier in this chapter that bad habits in the use of language were infectious. The pseudo-objectivity of the passive voice comes from the belief that scientific and technical writers should strive to be impersonal. But it also comes from a misunderstanding of how to be impersonal when using language. I am not necessarily being impersonal in the use of language when I avoid using words like *I*, *me* and *my*; I am merely being evasive. Young people are taught at school to say, for example, 'The apparatus was set up as shown in the diagram', and not, 'I set up the apparatus in the way the diagram shows'. But surely a statement like 'I set up the apparatus' is a statement of historical fact, and as objective and impersonal as a statement can be. At the same time it is an acknowledgement of the truth, for the apparatus could not have set up itself. It would become non-objective and personal only if certain kinds of modification, which described the writer's feelings, were introduced—if he said, for instance, 'I delightedly set up the lovely apparatus' or 'I reluctantly made a structure out of their filthy glassware'.

The point is that striving towards objectivity by using the passive voice leads to unreadable writing. And once started, the bad habit spreads. People who are not very good writers imitate others who are not very good either, and who have no deep understanding of how language works, and so a whole mass of turgid and stodgy prose is created.

4.3 Making the unreadable easily read

Any writer who sets out to tell other writers how to make their prose easily read finds himself in an invidious position. Let him who is without fault cast the first stone. The present writer is only too conscious of his own shortcomings. Nevertheless, he has had in his time been compelled to read a great deal of scientific and technical prose, and he has not always enjoyed it. He thinks that scientific and technical writers tend to make their sentences too long. He thinks that many of them show unnecessary wordiness or lack of conciseness. And he is always surprised that very few of them seem to be able to think clearly.

How short a short sentence might be is one of those questions like 'How long is a piece of string?' It is sometimes possible to make very long sentences quite easy to read. However, the report writer should try to keep his sentences reasonably short. Very easily read sentences are not more than ten to fifteen words long. A sentence of up to twenty-five words can normally be easily understood if the reader is acquainted with the subject-matter. When a sentence grows to thirty words it becomes difficult to understand, but may not be too difficult if the writer has managed it carefully. Sentences of more than thirty words should, in general, be avoided. They are to be found in the upper reaches of science and technology, in the language of the law, in documents like Acts of Parliament, and elsewhere. And they are sometimes necessary. But the report writer should think of his readers and try to make their job as easy as he can.

Unnecessary wordiness is not quite the same as the use of long words. Even so, a good writer will not use long words if he can find short ones. A long word is one of more than four syllables. A high proportion of long words in a sentence can make the sentence difficult to understand. But in scientific and technical writing there are some long words that cannot possibly be avoided. There is no substitute for *electrostatic* or *acceleration*. There can, of course, be no objection to the use of technical terms in scientific and technical writing. What is important is the way in which they are handled. But unnecessary wordiness is quite a different matter. It usually arises because the writer cannot come to grips with what he is talking about. This may be because, on the one hand, he wants to be impressive, and believes that in writing he must adopt a pompous and imposing style; or, on the other hand, he may be frightened of committing himself. He will say, for instance, 'Considerations have been given to the possibility that inimical meterological conditions might have a deleterious effect on the housing of the component', when he could say quite simply, 'I thought bad weather might harm it'. Or he might be too frightened to speak out, and so he says, 'It would appear to be likely from the already available evidence that the material will crack when cutting at high speeds takes place', instead of, 'It might crack when cut at high speed'.

As for the absence of clear thinking—we have already given some examples. It seems, very often, that technical and scientific writers fail to understand exactly what it is they have to say. They are well acquainted with their subject—perhaps too well acquainted—but cannot sort out their ideas so as to know which ideas to put down in their reports, and why those ideas and not any others.

We propose now to give some samples of bad English, and make suggestions for improvement. We should like to think that we are doing the same sort of thing as a report writer does when he revises. For clearly, a report writer will have to revise what he has written, and his revision can often turn a bad report into a good one.

Example (a)

The necessity for the complete reconstruction of the aerials and transmission lines at Stagby Radio Station, near Lincoln, has been brought about by the need to modernize equipment.

Opportunity has been taken to replace the old masts, which are upwards of 30 years old, by masts of a more modern design, and this should result in a considerable reduction of maintenance costs. The masts to be removed, 27 in number, are parallel-sided latticed-steel structures with a 12 ft square cross-section, each 290 ft high and weighing 33 tons.

This is a bad case of wordiness and confusion of thought making sentences too long.

Has the writer decided what he is talking about? Presumably, he is talking about the removal of the old masts and their replacement by new ones. But, if the old masts are to be replaced, they are not being reconstructed—*replacement* and *reconstruction* are not synonyms. It can only bewilder readers to tell them in the first sentence that one thing is happening, and then to contradict it in the second. If there is a need to modernize equipment, the new masts, one imagines, will be of 'a more modern design' than the old ones; it is not likely that obsolete equipment will be replaced by equipment even more obsolete. Consequently, why give useless information? And what about the second part of the second sentence? Is that information, expressed in two well-worn clichés, really relevant to what the writer is supposed to be talking about? What are we to make of such an expression as 'upwards of 30 years old'? Any number above 30 is 'upwards of 30', so we have no accurate information about the age of the masts; if it is necessary to say how old they are, why not give their exact age? And what about the expression '27 in number'? Everybody likely to read the report will know that 27 is a number, so why point out the obvious to them? Lastly, the use of the passive voice does not make the meaning clear; it comes from the starting of sentences with abstract words, *necessity* and *opportunity*, both of which dictate the sentence structure once they have been chosen, and neither of which is wanted. It is here that we can see again that the writer has not carefully thought out what he wants to tell the reader. If there is a need to modernize equipment, then there

will be a necessity to change some of it, and so there will be
no question of an opportunity being taken.

It seems it would be simpler to say, if the passive voice must
be kept:

In modernizing equipment at Stagby Radio Station, near Lincoln,
27 masts are being replaced. These masts are parallel-sided and
steel-latticed, with a 12 ft square cross-section. Each is 290 ft high
and weighs 33 tons.

Example (b)

Although the present standard of construction on main lines is, of
course, continuous welded rail, there are still large numbers of
fish-plated joints in existence and failure at the fishbolt holes con-
tinues to be the most frequent mode, both at the running-on end of
plain rails and on switch and crossing rails, especially wing rails.
This is because all these positions are liable to receive impact loads
from wheels more than twice as great as the static wheel load,
depending on the state of maintenance of the joint or crossing, the
speed of the trains, and the resilience of the ballast and formation.

Another important reason is because a bolt hole is a stress raiser
to the resolved maximum principal stresses acting along planes at
45 degrees to the horizontal in the web when a wheel rolls along
the rail.

These three long sentences, each of more than 30 words, are
used by the author to explain something quite difficult. The
length of the sentences increases the difficulty for the reader.
The unnecessary wordiness is due, again, to the author's not
having clearly thought out what the reader has to be told.

What does he want to say? First, the most frequent failures
in rails are at fishbolt holes. Second, the positions of the fishbolt
holes. Third, the reasons for failure.

Would it not have been best, therefore, for the author to have
planned his exposition on these lines?

As things are, the whole statement is confused. There seems
to be no reason for the first part of the first sentence which
says, 'Although the present standard of construction on main
lines is, of course, continuous welded rail.' The presence of
this clause only diverts the reader's attention from the main
theme, makes the sentence unnecessarily longer, and adds
nothing to the explanation of the failures. So, with that gone,

the second half of the first sentence can be clarified. Why say *large numbers of* when *many* would do? Does the phrase *in existence* serve any useful purpose? Could the word *mode* be got rid of?

The second sentence is even more confused. What are *wheels more than twice the weight of the static wheel load*? And what is it that depends on the state of maintenance—what is referred to by the pronoun *this*, or the fact that 'all these positions are liable to receive impact loads', or the failures, or the fact that the failures occur at fishbolt holes, or what? This reader has to confess that he does not know precisely what is the answer to this question. He assumes it is the fact that failures are likely to occur most frequently at fishbolt holes, but he cannot be certain. Presumably, if the joint or crossing is well maintained, if the speed of the trains is slow, and if the resilience of the ballast and the formation are as they should be, the risk of failure is reduced.

The third sentence starts off with a common, but not excusable, grammatical error which arises from lack of clear thinking. It is difficult to see how 'another important reason' can be 'because'. Surely what is stated in the clause beginning with *because* is another reason.

The writer of this book is not certain whether the following revision says what the original intended to say, but he gives it for what it is worth:

Most failures in fishplate-joined rails occur at the fishbolt holes at the running on ends of plain rails, and on switch and crossing rails, especially on wing rails. One reason is that these positions are liable to receive from moving wheels impact loads more than twice the weight of the static wheel load, according to the state of maintenance of the track, the speed of the trains, and the resilience of the ballast and formation. A second reason is that a bolt hole is a stress raiser to the resolved maximum principal stresses acting along planes at 45 degrees to the horizontal in the web when a wheel rolls along the rail.

Example (c)
Considerable interference with electrical installations and radio receivers located in the vicinity of VHF and UHF transmitting stations can be caused and to avoid the contingency of this interference the whole of the transmitting equipment necessitates being screened

in a conducting envelope which has subsequently to be efficiently earthed. Not infrequently copper spraying has been utilized to coat the whole of the interior of chambers, walls, floors and ceilings, of transmitting stations which, in conjunction with copper mesh over windows and copper sheeting on the doors, can form such a completely screened envelope. After spraying, normal decoration can be carried out either by means of painting, papering or plastering, the matt nature of the sprayed copper surface being an excellent bond for any such form of internal decoration.

Here is a sample of wordiness gone to excessive lengths. The result is that reading with clear understanding becomes difficult. The word *considerable* is often found in technical writing, and one often wonders what it means. It is a word used, one imagines, to mean 'much, many, or a lot of'. But exactly how much or how many is never stated. The word *located* turns up very often in the register of engineering, and no doubt it sometimes has a place there. But in the passage given above, the expression *located in the vicinity of* can only be viewed and heard with horror. Why not say *near*? The expression *to avoid the contingency of* is pompous wordiness gone mad. Moreover, the sudden transition to the second part of the long first sentence introduced by this expression makes it difficult for the reader to know where he stands. And *necessitates* is another of these pompous words which some people, trying to be impressive, make use of in trying to show off before their readers. The jingle of the sounds at the ends of the words *subsequently* and *efficiently* is also a fault of hasty and ill-considered writing distasteful to sensitive readers who like to hear the rhythms and sounds of words in sentences.

It is obvious that this first sentence of the passage is too long. What it says should either be given two sentences or else be very much simplified.

Another example of unnecessary wordiness that comes from failure to master what is being talked about is the apologetic use of the double negative *not infrequently*. What the author means, one imagines, is nothing more impressive than just the plain word *often*. Again, the word *utilized* is one that often turns up in technical literature, even though there is the simpler, and therefore better, word *used*. And why the author should say *chambers*, when he means *rooms*, is a mystery. So too is his use of *walls, floors and ceilings* when he has already said *the whole of the interior*—it seems pointless to tell his readers that walls, floors and ceilings are parts of rooms. Nor does the expression *the matt nature of*, which shows a misuse of the word *nature*, make the passage more lucid. If, after a surface has been sprayed, it has a matt finish, why not simply say so?

The passage could be revised in this way:

The equipment of VHF and UHF transmitters needs an earthed conducting screen to prevent its interfering with nearby electrical installations and radio receivers. Combined with copper mesh over windows and copper sheeting on doors, copper spraying is often used to coat all the interiors of transmitting stations. Rooms thus sprayed can be decorated normally, for the matt finish of a copper-sprayed surface is a good bond for paint, paper and plaster.

Reading these passages shows that it is always necessary for the report writer to have a very clear idea of what he wants to say before he starts his writing. All too often, one feels, technical and scientific writers blunder into the construction of their sentences before they have decided what the sentence is for, and what it is intended to do in the paragraph in which it occurs. This is not the way to produce clear and readable reports.

When the writer has made up his mind about what he wants to say, he should consider which is the best sentence pattern in which to say it. The first principle should be that of unity. That is, the sentence is about one topic and one topic only. The writer of (c) above, for instance, obviously packed too much into the first sentence of the passage. What exactly was his subject? Was it that VHF and UHF transmitters interfere with nearby electrical installations and radio receivers? Or was it that the equipment of such transmitters needs to be screened? Or was it that copper-spraying was a good way, in his opinion, of making such screens? It seems to be clear from the evidence of the passage that the writer had not thought out carefully the answers to some such questions as these. He started writing with the first thought that came into his head. The result was that he had to go on in the way in which this first thought dictated. Such a method is all right for producing the earliest draft of the finished composition. For some writers find that they can see what they have to say more clearly when they have put it down on paper. In the very earliest draft what has to be said can be put down in any higgledy-piggledy order that the writer cares to use. But it will not do for the final draft which is to be read by readers for whom the report is written.

The good report writer will therefore ask himself of every sentence that he writes: What is the topic—what is the sentence about? He will then ask himself: Is that topic relevant to the passage as a whole? If it is not, he should simply abandon it. If it is relevant, then the writer should ask himself what precisely he wants to say about the topic. What words are going to be chosen to name the topic and become the grammatical subject of the sentence? When he has decided on these words, he should think carefully about what is referred to by them does, did, or will do. This will lead him to the main verb of the sentence. What sort of a verb is it to be? Is it one that is subject-oriented? Is it one, like a part of the verb *to be*, that will make the sentence into a kind of definition? Or is it some kind of verb that will bring what is referred to by the subject into some relationship with something else, and if it is, what sort of relationship?

The writer will then have to think about whether what he has to say had better be said in the active or the passive voice. Should the leader of a research team, for instance, say, 'Methods of output of test data from the scale-friction dynamometer, and the subsequent time spent on interpretation, have been the subject of long discussion'? Or should he say, 'The team discussed at length the methods of output of test data from the scale-friction dynamometer and the time afterwards spent on interpretation'? And when, eventually, the writer has made all these decisions and written his sentence, he should go through it once more and check. If he finds he has written, 'The pressure signals from the chart recording of a fade and recovery cycle are transposed to a data tape, and with a suitable programme are fed into a computer', he should not necessarily be satisfied. Is the expression with *a suitable programme* really wanted? Obviously, no one is going to waste time on an unsuitable programme. And how is anything to be fed into a computer without a data tape? And could not the second *are* be omitted without loss of clarity?

If the report writer is to produce good work, he must give constant vigilance to every detail, no matter how minute it may seem.

4.4 Exposition and Cohesion

So far we have been talking about the use of English as it applies to the construction of sentences. But sentences normally exist in paragraphs, and the paragraphs exist in a complete composition. The two topics called Exposition and Cohesion deal with these matters. They deal with the assembling of paragraphs out of sentences, and of paragraphs considered in their relation to one another in the total piece of prose of which they are parts.

It is difficult to separate these two concepts. They exist, however, and can be discovered by the examination and analysis of all passages of well-written prose. Consider the following passage. It is taken from the autobiography of James Nasmyth, and gives a description of the Black Country as it appeared to Nasmyth in 1830:

The Black Country is anything but picturesque. The earth seems to have been turned inside out. Its entrails are strewed about; nearly the entire surface of the ground is covered with cinder heaps and mounds of scoriae. The coal, which has been drawn from below ground, is blazing on the surface. The district is crowded with iron furnaces, puddling furnaces, and coal-pit engine furnaces. By day and by night the country is glowing with fire, and the smoke of iron-works hovers over it. There is a rumbling and clanking of iron forges and rolling mills. Workmen covered with soot, and with fierce white eyes, are seen moving about amongst the glowing iron and the dull thud of forgehammers.

Amidst these flaming, smoky, clanging works, I beheld the remains of what had once been happy farmhouses, now ruined and deserted. The ground underneath them had sunk by the working out of the coal, and they were falling to pieces. They had in former times been surrounded by clumps of trees, only the skeletons of which remained, dilapidated, black, and lifeless. The grass had been parched and killed by the vapours of sulphureous acid thrown out by the chimneys; and every herbaceous growth was of a ghastly grey—the emblem of vegetable death in its saddest aspect. Vulcan had driven out Ceres. In some places I heard a sort of chirruping

sound, as of some forlorn bird haunting the ruins of the old farm-
steads. But no! the chirrup was a vile delusion. It proceeded from
the shrill creaking of the coal-winding chains, which were placed in
the small tunnels beneath the hedgeless road.

The first point to notice about this passage of prose is that it
has a unity. That is to say, it is about one topic and one topic
only. In general, it refers to the Black Country which Nasmyth
saw as a landscape in 1830.

Now it is quite obvious that about any subject millions of
statements can be made. An enormous number of facts could
be given, or an endless expression of ideas, beliefs, opinions,
points of view, feelings, emotions, and attitudes of mind all
about the subject could be set down. It is also obvious that in
a few hundred words and a dozen to fifteen sentences only a
small fragment of all that could be said can in fact be said.
Consequently, the author has to select. And what he selects for
any particular passage of prose is one fact, one idea, one
opinion, one belief, one point of view or whatever—and only
one, not more.

In the passage in question, Nasmyth has chosen to state that
in his opinion the Black Country is not picturesque. The passage gets its unity from the fact of this selection, because once
having started to express that opinion, Nasmyth keeps on with
it and refers to nothing else. He sets down what he sees, and
everything he sees provides evidence for the opinion which he
holds. And we know what this opinion is because it is stated
unambiguously in the first sentence of the passage.

The first principle of exposition, therefore, is to have a theme.
A theme of a passage of prose is its subject-matter. And it is
always possible to say what the subject-matter of a passage of
prose is. Therefore the theme can always be expressed in a
sentence which sums up what the passage is about, but which
sums it up in two ways. The first of these ways is to state the
general subject of the passage—to state what, from all the millions of subjects there are in the universe to talk about, precisely which of those millions of subjects has been selected. The
second of these ways is to state the *particular* subject of the passage—to state what, from all the millions of things that could
be said about the general subject, precisely has been selected
to say about that. In the passage in question, the general subject,

F

as we have hinted, is the Black Country which Nasmyth saw as a landscape in 1830—and millions of statements could have been made about the Black Country which Nasmyth saw. But the particular subject which Nasmyth chose was his opinion that the Black Country was not picturesque.

As we read through the passage, we notice that it has two paragraphs. And reading the first of these we can observe, if we look carefully, that a principle of continuity is present. In each sentence except the first, we can find a word which refers back, in some way or another, to the sentence before it. The technical name for this reference back is *anaphora*, and of anaphora there are three kinds—grammatical, lexical, and that belonging to register. An example of grammatical anaphora is seen in the word *its* which begins the third sentence. This word refers back to the word *earth* in the previous sentence, and thus joins the two sentences together, so that there is an easy transition from the thought of the second sentence of the paragraph to the third one. An example of lexical anaphora is seen in the use of words of allied but different meaning. There is a connexion between the meaning of the expressions *blazing on the surface* and *glowing with fire*, and between the word-groups *rumbling and clanking* and *dull thud*. These two pairs of expressions link together what is seen on the one hand, and what is heard on the other. An example of anaphora of register is found in the general use of words in the passage which refer to the same area of human experience. In the first paragraph we have such words as *coal, iron furnaces, puddling furnaces, forges, rolling mills*, and so on. In the second paragraph, in the anaphora of register, we have, first, such words as *farmhouses, clumps of trees, grass, herbaceous growth, bird*, which remind us of the countryside; and second, we have the words *ruined, falling to pieces, skeletons, delapidated, lifeless*, and so on, which suggest the notion that an old rural way of life is gone for ever.

If he looks carefully, the reader will be able to discover several more examples of these ways of ensuring the continuity of the train of thought throughout the passage. He will see that there is a consciously contrived method of linking idea to idea, sentence to sentence, so as to produce what is called cohesion. In other words, the unity and continuity of the passage combine to give this cohesion to it. Each separate utterance—sentence, clause, phrase or whatever it is—has its part to play in the total structure, and each has some reference *outside itself* to some other part of the total structure of words and sentences.

Moreover, the reader should also note that, although there is continuity throughout the whole passage, each of the two paragraphs is about a different topic. The first paragraph is about the evidences of industrialization which make the author believe that the Black Country is not picturesque; and the second one is about the evidences of the ruin of a former agricultural way of life which reinforce this impression. Thus the two paragraphs, though separate entities, have a cohesion of register—they are both about the same subject. Nor are they cut off linguistically. The first words of the second paragraph, *Amid these flaming, smoky, clanging works*, display both grammatical and lexical anaphora. The grammatical anaphora is seen in the word *these*, and the lexical anaphora in the words *flaming, smoky, clanging works*. All these words thus maintain the continuity of the piece at the same time as they provide a setting for what is to follow; and what is to follow flows naturally from the words *I beheld*.

From such examination and analysis of prose passages as this, we can deduce the principles behind good continuous writing, or what is usually called exposition, which is the art of setting out in the best way the ideas that a writer wants to express. We have already said that the first principle of exposition is to have a theme. What this amounts to is saying that before one can say anything one must have something to say, and that one must have a clear idea of what that something is; a clear selection must be made of one, and only one, notion, from all there is to select from. And if one has something to say, there must be a way of saying it if it is to get said at all. A good way of saying it is to follow the example of the best writers; and if one does not know who the best writers are, then one must rely on the knowledge and experience of those who, like the writer of this book, have spent a lifetime studying the subject.

The principles of good exposition can be summarized as:

Every well-written passage of prose will have a *theme*, which can be summarized in a sentence which declares both the general and the particular subject of the passage. This theme will then be expressed in paragraphs which have:

1. *Unity*—each paragraph will be about one topic and one topic only;
2. *Topic sentence*—a sentence, normally the opening one, which declares somewhere in it what the topic of the paragraph is;
3. *Planned arrangement*—the sentences inside the paragraph are consciously arranged, with grammatical and lexical cohesion and cohesion of register, so as to leave in the reader's mind an accurate impression of what the writer wants to say;
4. *Paragraph links*—the device of anaphora, grammatical or lexical or of register, should be used in all paragraphs except the first to ensure continuity from one paragraph to the next.

It should be clear from all this that exposition and cohesion are intimately connected; if one properly achieves the first one automatically achieves the second; and it is through an understanding of the second that one knows how to achieve the first.

We must now turn to another aspect of exposition. This aspect deals with the way in which the author's intentions influence the kind of sentence structure he uses. We mention this aspect so that the report writer may have an insight into the sort of things he is doing when he writes, and so that he can adjust the kinds of sentences he uses to making his meaning clear to his reader.

Consider the following paragraphs. They are extracts from a set of notes which an engineer made for a talk he had to give on noise and noise measurement.

GENERAL NOTES ON NOISE AND NOISE MEASUREMENT

1. Many years ago, when I was an apprentice, we never stopped to think, when we tackled problems of engine design, that we were pioneers who were creating the noisiest environment in the history of man. We knew that torsional vibration could make engines produce strange noises, that it could even make them seize up, or rattle the doors of the workshop or break windows or set tools dancing about on the benches. In this manner we learnt about critical speeds, so that we usually decided the critical speed of an engine by listening to it. We ran the engine up to its full-load speed, and if it made no queer noises, did not break its

crankshaft, and if the fabric of the workshop remained intact after a decent interval, we knew that the engine was all right. We have now advanced a great deal since those early days, and the noise emitted by engines of all kinds is becoming something of a national, even an international, nuisance.

2. A sound-level meter is a device which can be used to measure sounds in a variety of circumstances. It is used normally to measure the level of loudness, and the measurements may be made for a variety of reasons—to estimate the risk of damage to hearing, to estimate the annoyance or inconvenience a sound may cause, to evaluate the effectiveness of damping or some kind of accoustical treatment, or to compare different products. Basically, a sound-level meter is a microphone connected to an amplifier, a detector and a meter gauge. It usually indicates a root mean square in units of decibels, which are the units of the relative intensity of sound. A decibel is calculated as a logarithmic ratio of the sound pressure to that which is arbitrarily decided as the threshold of human hearing, that is, the pressure of the vibrations in the atmosphere on the human ear-drum at the lowest audible sound level. This value is 0.0002 dyn/cm^2. Such a scale is chosen because a source producing the same sound may vary its noise level in different circumstances. For instance, the diesel engine of a truck, running at the same number of revolutions a minute, could produce different noise levels in an enclosed shed, in a crowded city street, and on an open country road. Some sound-level meters are fitted with frequency selectors for analysing sound in spectra. Weighting circuits can sometimes be incorporated so that a meter reading approximating to the response of the human ear can be given.

3. Somebody once said that noise was unwanted sound. In other words, before noise can become a problem the sounds in the environment must become so great, or of such intensity, that they interfere with comfort, health and human happiness. But we experience noise as a sensation, and it is impossible to measure a sensation quantitatively. Still less is it possible to measure the value which individuals attach to certain sounds or to decide what is a sound and what is a noise in an individual's estimation. A young man may love the roar that comes from the exhaust of his sports car, but his grandmother may detest it.

4. Nevertheless, it is possible to make out a good case for the proposition that engineers should interest themselves in the problems of noise. And if there comes to be general agreement, as seems likely, that noise is unwanted sound, then it is clearly the engineers who will have to get rid of the unwanted, for nobody else

can. The source of sound is the movement of something transmitted through the medium of the air. The engineers of the world have been responsible, more than anybody else, for the design, production and distribution of things that move, and, as I suggested earlier, they have probably created, in the second half of the twentieth century, the noisiest environment in the history of man. This noise can only increase—or at least, the proliferation of possible sources of noise in the making of machines which move is not likely to diminish. Soon there will come a limit, nearly reached now in a busy London street, at which it will be impossible for people to hear one another speak in ordinary conversation. There is a responsibility on engineers to quieten the world down a bit. They can do this only by deeper and deeper investigation into the design of things that move—in particular, into the design of engines.

The reader is asked to look carefully through these four paragraphs, and especially to examine the verbs. He should try to see which of the verbs are subject-oriented and which are not. For example, in the first paragraph there is a larger proportion of verbs which are not subject-oriented than in the second paragraph, where most of the verbs are parts of the verb *to be*. But in the third and fourth paragraphs the verbs seem more mixed.

It is, as we have suggested, the verbs that mainly influence the sentence pattern. Generally speaking, we can say that those verbs which are subject-oriented indicate that the writer of the sentences in which they occur is imposing his thought on the world; he is dealing with mental events and ideas. On the other hand, in those sentences in which the verbs are not subject-oriented, the writer is objectively describing or recounting events in the outside world. The use of the passive voice is an effort to make the former of these ways of speaking out of the latter, since only sentences which have non-subject-oriented verbs can be expressed in the passive.

The point is that in each of the four paragraphs given above the writer is doing something different. In the first paragraph he is narrating, that is, setting down a string of events. He is answering the question, What happened? The result is that he is constantly bringing the people referred to by the pronoun *we* into relationships with something else. These people 'tackled problems', or 'learnt about critical speeds', and they were aware that 'engines produced strange noises'; they listened;

and they knew something about engines. But in the second paragraph, the author is describing. So that in this paragraph events rarely happen. Instead, things *are*. That is why parts of the verb *to be* predominate. The subject-matter is what a sound-level meter is and what it consists of. Consequently, the thing referred to has no activity; it remains inert and passive while the author examines it. Suddenly, however, towards the end of the second paragraph, the author gives an example; to do this he has to turn away from the description of a passive object, so that he can show something doing something: it is the diesel engine producing noise. At this moment, the kind of sentence pattern changes. In the third paragraph, the author is again doing something different. He is explaining. Explanation usually answers some such question as: How does it come about that such-and-such happens or is so? In this case, the author is explaining how it comes about that noise is different from sound. Consequently, he has both to narrate and describe, and therefore, his sentence patterns become mixed; some of them are subject-oriented and some of them are not. The same sort of thing happens in the fourth paragraph as happens in the third, but in a slightly different way. In the fourth paragraph, the author is presenting his readers with an argument, and arguments normally concern questions of belief or opinion. We cannot say that narration is a matter of belief or opinion, since narration is writing which at least assumes the existence of historical fact, although, of course, some narration may be fiction and some may be delusion. Nor can we say that description is opinion or belief; when the author says that a sound-level meter is a microphone connected to an amplifier and to a detector and a meter gauge, we again accept what he says as fact. And explanation too starts with the existence of physical fact, for if explanation sets out to answer some such question as how does it happen that such-and-such happens or is so, then we have no alternative but to accept the existence of such-and-such. Types of writing like narration, description and explanation usually and normally have a context found for them by the writer's observations of the external world. But an argument is a piece of writing that starts with a concept and not with an objective fact. As the author says, sound and noise are experienced as physical sensations, and as such they are facts of the external universe distinct from conceptual relationships. But the proposition that the engineer should interest himself in the problems of noise is entirely an idea thought up in the mind, and not a fact of physical and perceptual experience, like the experience of sound. In this way, a piece of writing which presents an argument is likely to be one which provides its own context; and it is likely to present thoughts and ideas which readers may or may not agree with.

The notions of exposition which we have tried to set out in this section bring us in touch with a few, though by no means all, of the finer points of good writing. We mention them because we think that they should help the report writer to be aware of what he is doing when he is writing. And if he can have some insight into what he is doing with every sentence that he writes, know what every sentence has to contribute to every paragraph, and how the coherence of the whole work is achieved, then he can produce writing which is readable.

In the end, the report writer will find as he gains experience of his craft that there are no fixed and rigid rules which can produce good writing. There are certain conventions and usages which he can imitate and adhere to, just as, in all forms of civilized intercourse among men, there are certain standards of behaviour which are acceptable; and there are certain restraints upon the uninhibited originality of individuals which have to be imposed if human intercourse is to be possible at all. But eventually the report writer will find that he is usually expressing himself, and that he is a unique individual with his own personality. He may submerge this personality, if he wishes, under a mass of clichés and well-worn means of expression that can be found every day in the uninspired writing in thousands of reports in technical journals; but this seems to be a negative approach to writing which can only lead to the writer's stultifying and limiting his personality instead of expanding and realizing it. Sooner or later, the writer will find that he is left to his own resources, that he has to make his own decisions, that no one can help him except himself.

4.5 Correctness and Convention

A report writer is not a free man. He is always bound and re-

stricted in what he does by the fact that a report exists solely
for the sake of its readers who have to read the report in the
line of duty. If the report writer were a poet or a novelist, he
could express himself with comparative freedom, and could be
entitled to expect that at least some of his readers might come
more than half-way to meet him. For the creative writer is a
man who can take a great deal of pleasure in experiment, and
who can explore all the resources of the language in new and
exciting ways to discover what words and sentences can do.
Unfortunately, the report writer is denied this privilege. He
must be content with the more humdrum, but nevertheless important, usefulness of simple and unpretentious prose. He must
always remember that the request for a report normally comes
from those who employ him, that those who want to read what
he has to say are busy men and women with a job of work to
do, and that the duty he owes to his readers must for ever be
his first concern.

The two notions of correctness and convention are relevant
here. Correctness in writing is a concept which covers and
describes an established set of rules that have grown up over
the years among the educated and the cultured; such rules
are found to be convenient in normal linguistic intercourse
among civilized people, because when people observe them
other people know what is meant, and communication is thus
made easier. The prearrangement of the code is kept intact, and
everybody knows where he stands. Convention is merely ad-
herence to these rules in normal practice. So convention, in this
sense, comes to refer to ordinary good manners.

Nevertheless, in spite of the existence of these two notions, and
in spite of the fact that some people, apparently, will always
insist that such-and-such a usage is the 'correct' one, there is
always the likelihood of some disagreement. For instance, as I
write these words I have on my desk two booklets. One is
called *Notes for Authors* and is issued by the Institute of Physics;
the other, issued by the Chemical Society, is called *The Presentation of Papers to the Chemical Society*. In the first booklet it is
stated categorically, page 20: 'The ending -ize, *not* -ise, should
be used in such words as "realize", "recognize", "economize",
where the suffix "ize" derives from the Greek . . .' But the
other booklet, page 12, says less peremptorily: 'Each of the

forms "-ise," "-ize," and their derivatives, is permitted, provided that consistency is maintained throughout . . .' It seems odd that physicists should have to confine themselves to one form, and that chemists can be more free. After all, the decision to use one or the other form is quite arbitrary, and I should say the decision is one that each writer should make for himself. Surely if a man can be educated enough to be able to produce original work in physics, he ought to be able to spell. (The reader should note, too, the use of the comma after the examples in the two quotations just given; while the writer of this book would not go to the same lengths as the physicists about the use of *-ize/-ise*, he must say that the chemists' use of the comma inside the inverted commas seems to be quite irrational, since the inverted commas are intended to set apart what is to be considered, of which the comma is not a part.)

We now propose to give some guides to writers on what might be called correct and conventional usage. But as we have just shown, there is no absolute agreement. The author of this book can only give his own views. With those people who think he is wrong he is quite happy to agree to differ. He does not want to be dogmatic.

Spelling

The author has found one good rule about spelling, which he has steadfastly followed throughout his career as a writer, and which has never let him down. It is this: When in doubt, consult the *Oxford English Dictionary*. Life can be as simple as that. And to those people who say that they have no *Oxford English Dictionary*, the author's reply is: Get one.

In general, the advice of the chemists given above seems reasonable. If there are two ways of spelling a word, choose one and stick to it. 'Provided that consistency is maintained throughout', it does not matter which is chosen. The author of this book would always write *-ize* where that suffix 'derives from the Greek'; but one does not always expect other people to know as much Greek or etymology as oneself, and so one is not unduly perturbed when one reads that 'Best equalised in the 29th minute'.

Abbreviations

The first rule about abbreviation is: Do not abbreviate at all unless there is some overwhelming necessity or one is writing highly technical matter and using the names of units for which there is an agreed or conventional abbreviated form.

Certainly one does not abbreviate words used in the course of ordinary continuous prose. It is said that one should not, if one is polite, abbreviate the names of the months in dates: one should write *4th* (or simply *4*) *November 1970*, and not *4th Nov. 1970*. It is also said not to be polite to abbreviate such words as *Street, Road, Square*, etc. in addresses.

Abbreviations in common use, like *Mr* for *Mister* and *Mrs* (pronounced 'missis') for *Mistress*, have become established as forms of title, and there is, of course, no reason to alter them. They should not be written with a point or full stop after them. The general rule about a full stop after an abbreviation is this: if the abbreviation is made from the first and last letters of the full word, as with *Mr* and *Mrs*, there is no need for a full stop; if the abbreviation is the first letter or first few letters of the full word, as with *U.S.* for *United States*, or *temp.* for *temperature*, then the full stop is needed—*except for the names of units in scientific and technical writing*. There is one exception to this exception, and that is with *in.* for *inch* or *inches* when it could be confused with the pronoun *in*; although when it occurs in such an expression as *lb/in²* there is obviously no need for the full stop.

In scientific and technological writing hundreds of abbreviations have come to be used as words in their own right. It is only to be expected that scientists and engineers, in developing their concepts and skills, should also develop a terminology to deal with them. And since so much of science and its applications are based on mathematics, it is clear that there should have been a tendency to abbreviate the names of units when calculations were being made. If the report writer has to use the names of these units, there is, of course, no objection to his using the abbreviations for them, provided that his readers can understand what he is doing.

For a complete list of the abbreviations of the names of units of measurement, and for examples of standard abbreviations for words other than the names of units (such as *conc.* for *concentrated* or *r.m.s.* for *root mean square*), the reader should refer to the British Standards Institution booklet, *Letter Symbols, Signs and Abbreviations*, BS 1991. If he is concerned with American usages, he should also refer to the American Standards Association's *Abbreviations for Scientific and Engineering Terms (210.1)*.

There is one final rule: do not add -*s* to form the plural of an abbreviation.

Numbers

The only rules about numbers and numbering can be observed from practice, and that seems to be chaotic. Here are one or two general guides, based on common sense.

For numbers below ten, use words rather than numerals. However, this may sometimes lead to oddities, as when two numbers come together. Some such expression as '16 4 B.A. bolts secure the back-plate' might confuse some readers and it would be better to write *sixteen* instead of '16'.

Do not use numerals to begin a sentence. An utterance like '5000 indexed operations were recorded during a normal day shift' is both confusing and offensive to the eye of the reader. It would be better to start with the phrase, 'During a normal day shift . . .'

Definite guidance does exist for expressing large numbers and the decimal marker. For example,

$$68\ 743{\cdot}75$$

is preferred to

$$68,\ 743{\cdot}75$$

Commas should not be used to separate groups.

For quantities smaller than unity, a cipher should always precede the decimal marker. For example

$$0{\cdot}329 \text{ not } {\cdot}329$$

The writer of technical reports will be well advised to consult BS 1991 for a full explanation of such general rules and for specific guidance in expressing mathematical symbols and signs, physical quantities, units and abbreviations.

Do not use numerals for estimated numbers. That is, say 'Approximately five hundred cases were salvaged from the fire.'

Do not use numerals for ordinals. Say, 'This is the fifth failure reported in four weeks.'

Quotation marks

As we saw in the quotations given earlier in this section, there is some doubt, even among those who lay down the law about writing technical papers, about how quotation marks should be used.

Printers, who are highly skilled craftsmen and who like to produce work which is pleasing to the eye, say that an excessive use of points spoils the appearance of a page. The author of this book agrees with them. Quotation marks are offensive. They should be abolished. Like chewing-gum and the drinks one gets from vending machines, which the author also detests, they are among the more disagreeable of modern inventions. The Authorized Version of the Bible did very well without them.

The author recommends that single quotation marks should be used for most quotations, and double quotation marks only for quotations inside single quotation marks.

Sometimes an unusual word, or a word used in an unusual sense, is put inside inverted commas:

> Water-cooled "lances" are introduced into the furnace at very high temperatures.

These so-called lances are apparently copper rods. This practice seems highly undesirable. Why not call things by their proper names?

As to whether a comma or a full stop comes before or after the inverted commas, there is little doubt in the author's mind about what the correct usage should be. If we were writing the dialogue for a novel, we should put the commas and full stops inside the quotation marks: 'Sir Jasper,' said Margarite icily, 'you may take from me my wealth and position, but never my honour.' But if we were genuinely quoting, and not just writing *oratio recta*, we would do the opposite:

> We have defined the word *code*, on an earlier page in this book, to mean 'a finite set of prearranged signs for making signals'.

Further, if we had been the writer of the quotations given on pages 83 and 84, we should not have put the words *realize*, etc., or the suffix *-ize*, in quotation marks. We should have asked our typist to underline them, and when they got printed they would have been in italics.

Hyphens

On the whole, we think the same about hyphens as we think about quotation marks—the fewer they are, the better we like them. However, they are necessary to avoid ambiguity. There is no need to write *cathode-ray* when *cathode* is an adjective modifying the word *ray*. Leave the hyphen out if you are talking about cathode rays. But when the whole compound becomes an adjective in its own right, as in the expression *cathode-ray tube*, then the hyphen can be permitted to stay.

The general rule should be to keep the hyphenated compounds as adjectives, and only to use the hyphen in a noun compound when there is a well established case, as with *subject-matter* or *blotting-paper*.

Certainly, we must use hyphens for adjectival numbers, as in *the fifty-two weeks of the year*. And we must use them too in those words in which the first part of the compound cannot stand as a word by itself, as with *infra-red* or *ultra-violet*. And we must also suppose that a distinction has to be made between *co-ordinate* as a verb in common usage and the noun *coordinate* of the mathematicians. It is regrettable that *horse-power*, with its hyphen, has come to stay, but it is not so regrettable to note that *gramme-molecule* is giving way to its official abbreviation *mole*.

Grammar

Solecisms, or offences against the grammatical conventions, are not so much reprehensible in themselves as in what they display of the attitude to the language of those who commit them. If a man who sets out to write does not show some respect for his medium, he immediately condemns himself in the eyes of the people who have to read what he has written.

Without doubt, the most common grammatical error to be found in technical and scientific writing is the use of the unrelated participle. It can lead even men with higher degrees into producing the most outrageous nonsense:

> Thompson found, after being immersed in the solution for 60 minutes, certain abnormalities appeared in the electrode.

One can well imagine it. Thompson should have immersed the electrode in the solution and not himself. Say, 'Thompson found

that certain abnormalities appeared in the electrode after it
had been immersed in the solution for 60 minutes'.

> Moving the workpiece relative to the beam, the sodium chloride
> lens was found not to focus on the required part of the surface.

One can hardly believe that the lens itself moved the workpiece
relative to the beam, and—incidentally—one imagines that the
lens was used to focus the beam and not itself on the part of
the surface the beam was supposed or intended to focus on. It
would presumably be impossible to say in technical writing, 'I
moved the workpiece relative to the beam, but still could not
get the lens to focus the beam on the right spot', so one would
have to say, 'The sodium chloride lens did not focus the beam
on the right part of the surface, even when the workpiece was
moved'.

> Having detected the error the problem was to correct it, whether
> manually or by re-sending the data.

This horrible sentence should never have been written by an
educated man. The problem did not detect the error. Presumably the problem was which to do, correct the mistake
manually or resend the data. Say, 'When we found the mistake,
we had to correct it either manually or by resending the data.'
Pronouns misused can also be a fruitful source of grammatical
mistakes. There is, for instance, the impersonal *it* which can
sometimes run amok in an utterance and do it irreparable
damage.

> Based on the experience gained from these prototypes, it was
> decided to rebuild the housing of the sectional plates it had been
> decided to use in the first place.

What that means can only be guessed at. Normally, there is
only one prototype; any other examples of the same thing are
copies or imitations.
The word *this* can occasionally cause difficulties.

> Final separation is accomplished by a bag filter. This enables the
> gas to be freed and diverted to steam-heat the rest of the plant.

What enables the gas to be freed—the final separation, its
being accomplished or the bag filter?

Comparison is a mental process which technical writers apparently find difficult to manage.

> Preliminary calculations have shown that compared with 1963 the freight traffic on Soviet Railways by 1970 will increase by about 32 per cent as compared with 20 per cent for passenger traffic.

How can one compare the year 1963 with the freight traffic on Soviet Railways? And how many comparisons are being made? Is the total amount of traffic for 1963 being compared with the estimated total for 1970, or the amount of freight traffic with the amount of passenger traffic?

> Comparison of the data demonstrated that the quantities of flake graphite in test bars H and G were greater than B or D.

One doubts whether the data were compared. Presumably the test bars were, and the experimenter found that there was more flake graphite in test bars H and G than in test bars B and D. Certainly the flake graphite was not compared with test bars B and D, though the sentence says it was.

The word *lesser* is also a source of confusion, especially when it turns up in such expressions as *to a lesser extent* or *to a lesser degree*. Nobody should allow his pen or typewriter to set down these expressions.

> Flashovers have increased in rarity on sections with electric traffic, and to a lesser degree on sections with diesel locomotives, whereas steam from steam locomotives caused flashovers to a much greater extent even with the new insulator specification.

The reader might like to attack this sentence for himself, if he thinks it is worthwhile. Steam damaged insulators, even those made to a new specification. This damage caused flashovers. Fewer steam locomotives meant less steam, and therefore less damage and fewer flashovers.

The misuse of *due to* and *owing to* is likely to upset the sensitive and damn the writer as a careless user of the language. Never, in any circumstances whatsoever, begin a sentence with '*Due to* . . .' The expression *due to* is an adjectival one and should only occur, if at all, after a part of the verb *to be*. You can say, if you must, 'These failures were due to inadequate storage', but 'Due to inadequate storage while the site was being prepared, the tubes failed again and again during construction' is horrible. Say, 'The tubes often failed during construction because they were not stored properly'.

In this connexion, many technical and scientific writers seem to find difficulty with reasons.

> Due to delays in the development of suitable refractory bats and because of the apparently greater market demanded, the prototype kiln has been set up initially for tile firing with the intention of converting it later to firing with carriet bats.

And what is one to make of that? Can the reader easily understand at first glance why the kiln has been made in that way?

Diction

Diction is a name used to cover the choice of words by a writer.

Some writers seem to think that the longer the word is the better it will serve their purpose. Other writers seem to prefer to choose other people's words and not think for themselves. They seem also to choose the longer and apparently more impressive words. In this way many unpleasant usages of words and expressions creep into the language of technical writing. Unfortunately, they do very little to clarify what the writer is talking about. The result is the creation of a jargon.

> That the overall picture suggests no imminent crisis in chemistry is not to say that the education sector is free from "internal imbalances".

What sort of a picture is an overall one? And what exactly is meant by the expression *imminent crisis in chemistry*? Presumably chemistry is a body of scientific knowledge, and as such is in no danger of being at any moment in a critical state. There might be a shortage of trained chemists, or the ways in which chemists are educated in chemistry may, in the author's opinion, be at fault, or there might be difficulties among chemists in the organization of their professional duties, or something like that. But to use the word *chemistry* to cover in that way the activities of chemists seems to be silly. One might also ask for a more precise definition of *the education sector*.

> Because it permits of the improved utilization of personal this procedure has been a major contributory factor in increasing the throughput of the plant.

G

What does the writer mean? If he means, 'Doing the job this way was helpful in speeding up production because it used manpower economically', why not say so?

> The submersile work chamber will overcome the two main problems currently experienced in diving operations in deep waters. These problems concern the diver's safety and dependence on weather conditions.

One does not overcome problems; one solves them. The word *currently* presumably means 'now'. And does one experience problems? Or how do problems concern something?

The use of abstract nouns is a cause of verbiage which affects clarity and purity of diction.

> Difficulty was experienced during the course of the investigations in finding a substance of sufficient purity other than the readily obtainable commercial grade product.

Why not say, 'I could not find a substance pure enough'?

> The realization of an efficient transportation system along with a satisfactory materials flow is an essential desideratum in any modern weaving plant.

Apart from the unpleasant sound made on the mental ear by the words *realization* and *transportation*, the fact that they are abstract nouns confuses the sentence. A desideratum is a felt want, or something missing. To say that a disideratum is essential therefore confuses the sentence even more. Why not say, if the obvious must be said, 'Materials must be moved efficiently in a modern weaving plant'?

One could go on for ever, and still find example after example of unfortunate English in technical and scientific literature. It is better in the end to try to offer something positive. At the beginning of this century, two brothers, H. W. Fowler and F. G. Fowler, gave this piece of advice: 'Any one who wishes to become a good writer should endeavour, before he allows himself to be tempted by the more showy qualities, to be direct, simple, brief, vigorous and lucid.' They added five practical rules:

> 'Prefer the familiar word to the far-fetched.
> Prefer the concrete word to the abstract.

Prefer the single word to the circumlocution.
Prefer the short word to the long.
Prefer the Saxon word to the Romance.'

The book from which these words are taken, *The King's English*, has been often recommended; it can be found in many libraries; and most teachers of English have passed on some of its contents to their pupils. Yet, as we have seen, people still go on ignoring these simple rules. Why?

Chapter five:
Extra-linguistic Material

5.1 Extra-linguistic Material

Ordinary language is the main tool of communication of the report writer. Most of what he has to say will be said in words and sentences. However, there may be occasions when he wants to supplement the language with communication of a different kind, even though there is some doubt in the minds of some people about whether he should or not. For some people think of tables, graphs and illustrations as devices which can divert the reader from the main text, make him forget what the main text is about, or interrupt the flow of thought which the main text has begun.

Clearly, there are many kinds of reports, and most of them, one would say, can manage to be effective without any use of extra-linguistic material at all. And most report writers are not competent to produce good illustrations to qualify for a place in the technical literature that gets printed and published. Most plans and drawings are done by experts; and in those firms and organizations which print and publish technical literature either get an agency which specializes in such work to do it for them or else have a trained staff of technical authors.

Clearly, too, the writer of a report must be very convinced that his report needs such extra-linguistic material before he thinks of using it. For such material is not a frilly extra which it might be nice to have but which could be dispensed with. If it is to be in the report at all it must convey information which cannot be conveyed in any other way. The report writer should therefore think very seriously about the need for this extra-linguistic material and the job he intends it to do. Naturally, his first thought will be that of the effect on his readers. If the extra-linguistic material will explain and illuminate for them parts of the report which cannot otherwise be explained and illuminated, then he must use it. But he should, generally speaking, try to use words and sentences to say what he has to say and not turn to graphs, tables and pictures as an easy way out.

Nevertheless, the value of some extra-linguistic material in some circumstances should not be underestimated. Tables can usefully display summaries of statistical information better than anything else, and can also set out some kinds of facts for quick and easy comparison. Graphs can show mathematical functions, and can also summarize statistics and details of quantities. Drawings and diagrams are sometimes useful to show the relative positions of components in some assemblies, or the essential details of some apparatus or equipment, which it might be tedious to explain and the explanation of which might be difficult to understand.

There are four questions to consider: how to present mathematics; what is a good table; what is a good graph; and what can be done with illustrations generally.

5.2 Mathematics

The first point to note about the inclusion of mathematically expressed formulae and equations in reports is that they are only likely to be read and understood by mathematicians or readers with sufficient mathematical knowledge to find them intelligible. The writer should therefore hesitate before he puts them in his report, and if he decides eventually that they must go in, he must choose carefully where. If they are to appear in the main discussion, then they must be clearly displayed. But it is often better to give only the main conclusions in the body of the report, and present the mathematical calculations in an appendix, to which those who want them may turn if they wish.

The second point to consider is the presentation. Obviously, great care has to be taken with the writing of mathematics. If the report has to be typed, and reports usually have, the writing of mathematics may present some difficulties. Standard typewriters have no characters for indices and subscripts, the Greek alphabet or special symbols. This is why, if the mathematics is of any great length, it is better to relegate it to an appendix. In this way it can be written carefully in longhand by the report writer and then photocopied. The printing of mathematics in books and journals needs a variety of type faces and special blocks.

The writer should make sure that the units and symbols used are standardized and consistent. (British Standard 1991 is used throughout Britain and is based on internationally accepted usages.)

All symbols that use horizontal bars can be used freely in longhand, but should not be used if the work has to be printed. Thus, write $\sqrt{ax^2 - b}$ in longhand if necessary, but $\sqrt{}(ax^2 - b)$ for the printer.

Algebraic fractions which appear in the main part of the text should be shown that they are so by means of a solidus and not with a horizontal bar. Thus, it is better to write $(a - b)/y$, and not $\dfrac{a - b}{y}$. However, the writer must be careful here and remember the brackets, for the solidus links only the two symbols next to it. The expression $a - b/y$ means $a - \dfrac{b}{y}$, not $\dfrac{a-b}{y}$.

If, however, the expression is more complicated and contains more than one fraction, it should be displayed; that is, it should be set out with a line all to itself, and the bar will indicate the fractions:

$$\frac{ax + b}{cx + d} = \frac{mx - p}{qx + r}$$

The same kind of display will have to be used for equations or expressions containing summation, product and integration symbols generally.

With simple numerical calculations and expressions there is not a great deal of difficulty. Most standard typewriters can cope with simple fractions like $\frac{1}{4}$, $\frac{1}{2}$, $\frac{3}{4}$, and many used in commercial offices have a longer range. Other numerical fractions can be dealt with by means of a solidus, as with $31/43$. The multiplication sign $\times$ should be used to express numerical products, since a full stop could be mistaken for a decimal point.

5.3 Tables

Tables are best used when there is a great deal of information to be presented, and readers can compare with ease the different items set out. For tables are givers of comparative information; they compare or contrast this with that.

However, what is meant by 'a great deal of information' is a question that needs to be carefully considered. Generally speaking, a great deal means three or more items of the same kind of information. A number of tests on materials intended to be used for the same purpose could have their results set out in a table, for instance; or the properties of some products to be compared could be tabulated. In such cases as these, the report writer will choose only the relevant information and present that; not all the results of all the tests would always need to be given.

The same sort of problem about the actual presentation of tables arises as with presenting mathematics. Tables should be prepared with a view to their being reproduced on a standard typewriter, since they may have to be cyclostyled or duplicated in some other form. Consequently, the tables should not be too large. Some large tables, such as those found in the *Monthly Bulletin of Statistics*, may sometimes be needed as a record, but the report writer should generally use small tables; the tables have to display information which can be quickly and easily grasped.

Tables can be set out in two ways, vertically and horizontally. Vertical tables are those displayed and readable when the page is in the normal position for reading. Horizontal tables are those which do not fit into the width of the page but which run over its length. If the table has to be so big that it will not fit on to the page at all, then it is too big. Such enormous tables may be needed occasionally, and may need special paper to set them out on. In that case, they will have to be inserted into the report and folded over; after it has been typed but such tables are inconvenient and cumbersome.

Obviously, vertical tables are most convenient for the reader. However, vertical tables should normally be set out to cover as much of the width of the page as possible without overshooting the margins.

Each table should have a heading. This should be presented in the form:

Table 6. Tensile Test Results of Electron-beam Welding

The columns should be arranged in what is the most natural order for reading them. Since tables compare and contrast, the names of what is being compared and contrasted should appear in the left-hand column, and the properties, qualities, findings, results, and so on, in the other columns. Each column should have a brief heading. In choosing and arranging the column headings, the report writer should bring related information together. If his table sets out information about air-conditioning equipment, for instance, all the information about, say, oil-wetted filters should appear in neighbouring columns. The vertical lines separating the columns should be set well apart so that the headings can be printed horizontally, and readers do not have to turn the page to right or left to read them.

The heading of a vertical table should appear at the top. But for a horizontal table the heading should be underneath. It should be written at the edge of the page which is nearer to the reader when he turns it.

Since most comparisons and contrasts will be made as a results of measurements, it is most important that all units should be stated. Needless to say, they should also be homogeneous. There is no point in giving metric units in one set of measurements and British standard units in another.

The contents of tables, and what precisely is to be compared and contrasted, should be thought out carefully. It should also be the least possible consistent with the information it is desired to give. Generally speaking, tables should present conclusions, that is, the results of investigations of some kind or another. They should summarize and display these conclusions for easy comparison. The readers of tables in reports are likely to use them as a basis for making decisions. Such decisions will be made on final results, and not on the means by which the final results were reached.

Tables can present information which would be tedious to read and even confusing if it were set out in continuous prose.

Table 1   Comparison of Average Salaries of Graduate Scientists in Five Disciplines for Financial Year ending 5th April 1969

Discipline	Age group								
	< 26	26–30	31–35	36–40	41–45	46–50	51–55	56–60	60–65
	£	£	£	£	£	£	£	£	£
Biology	1350	1600	2030	2300	2560	2995	3050	3075	4000
Chemistry	1290	1660	2100	2510	2950	3100	3175	3300	3700
Mathematics	1290	1895	2350	2575	3000	3200	3000	3400	3400
Metallurgy	1290	1600	1900	2400	2670	2950	3100	3125	2700
Physics	1350	1800	2175	2600	2975	3250	3440	3500	3500

They also present details which have to be compared, and they can make the act of comparison easy. The figures set out above can be seen almost at a glance, whether the comparisons are made vertically or horizontally.

Table 2   Comparison of Five New Dyestuffs introduced in March 197–

Name	Class	Uses	Light fastness	Wet fastness
1 Plocon blue	Reactive	Printing and dyeing acetates, polyesters pcv	Good	Medium
2 Nyquel Orange	Reactive	Cellulosics	High	High
3 Palino reds	Disperse	Dyeing wool, silk cellulosics, most blends	Very high	High
4 Cobrow blue	Disperse	Tri-acetate, pcv, polyesters	High	Medium
5 Torquol yellow	Reactive	Wool, silk, most blends, cotton	Medium	Medium

This table shows another way in which information can be compared. The information is not numerical, but the facts can be set out and seen at a glance.

5.4 Graphs

It is easy for the report writer to set out mathematics or to prepare tables by himself. But this is not normally so with graphs and illustrations, for these need a specialist art draughtsman if the work is to be reproduced. The report writer should always ask himself whether he really needs graphs and drawings to present what he has to say, and only use them if there is no other way out, for they can be troublesome and expensive to reproduce. In some firms and research organizations there is often a specialist staff employed to do the job, and if there is the report writer's task is to indicate precisely what he wants and leave the work to the experts.

First, the report writer must decide what the graph is intended to show and what has to be shown must be presented in a graph. Normally a graph can show mathematical functions or the relationships of a dependent to an independent variable. Graphs should, on the whole, be included in reports only for this purpose.

Clearly of importance is the choice of the scale and the size of the graticule. The point is that only the information part of the curve has to be shown—some mathematical functions can extend to infinity, but all that the reader of the report wants to know is the significant parts of the data he is presented with. As the reader can find out by experiment, changes in scale may alter the appearance of the curve, and the appearance of the curve would normally be what the report writer wants to present. The size of the graticule, taken in relation to the scale, can also affect the appearance of the curve—it can make it too large or too small; if the curve is too large, too much information may be presented and the significant detail lost to the reader, and if the curve is too small some of the significant detail may be lost because it does not appear at all.

When plotting a curve for reproduction by a specialist art draughtsman, the report writer should use graph paper of standard size, or should draw the graph to a scale large enough to be reduced easily. That is, he should estimate how much space the graph will occupy in the finished report, and then make his graph of a size of some easily understood multiple of this. When the draughtsman has to reduce its size, he does not want to have to choose an awkward scale to be able to do so; for if he has to choose an awkward scale there is the risk of error. The wise report writer would consult with the draughtsman, if he can, about this problem.

There is no need, in most cases, to give the small detailed grid of a graph. All that is wanted is the multiple units. These should generally be a multiple or sub-multiple of 10. The aim should be to give the minimum of grid lines consistent with making the graph intelligible.

The same sort of ideas about vertical and horizontal tables apply to graphs. The report writer should choose for preference a scale to make the graph fit neatly on the page when the page is in the normal reading position. But the graph itself should not have a tall thin appearance. Ideally, the abscissa or horizontal axis should always be slightly longer than the vertical axis. This is because the shape of what may be called a horizontal rectangle with a curve or curves inside it can be more easily read than that of what may be called a vertical rectangle.

The normally adopted convention is for the dependent variable to be plotted against the vertical or y-coordinate, and the independent variable on the abscissa.

Because the zero point on the coordinates of a graph in most cases appears at the bottom left-hand corner of the graph, a graph is normally read upwards. Therefore, the legend or title of the graph should normally appear underneath it. The title should take the form:

> Figure 2. Variation of Weber's constant with temperature for commercial sample of cadmium (Cd_1) and refined sample (Cd_2)

Any notes or supporting information, if necessary, should be written under the title, with each item, if there is more than one, numbered. But normally a good graph should be able to speak for itself; if it cannot, why use it?

The units should always be stated, and the writing which states them should always, if possible, be set out parallel to the top of the page, so that there is no need for the reader to turn the page through ninety degrees or put his head on one side to read it. On the graph whose title has just been given, for example, the units of temperature would be represented on the abscissa; therefore, immediately under the numbers at the bottom of each vertical grid line should appear a legend stating what the numbers are units of—for instance: Temperature °C. This legend can appear either in the middle or on the right-hand side. At the top of the y-coordinate, above the numbers at the left-hand ends of the horizontal grid lines, should be the

legend stating what these numbers represent—something like:
Weber's constant W. On the graph itself, which in this imaginary
case will have two curves presented for comparison, it is necessary, of course, to identify for readers which curve is which. So
at the upper limits of the curves would appear, for each curve
respectively, the symbols Cd_1 and Cd_2. If it can possibly be
avoided, no other writing should appear within the area of the
grid lines.

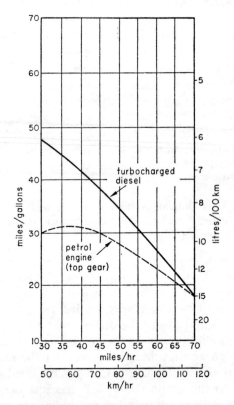

Figure 1 Fuel consumption at constant speeds of petrol and turbocharged
diesel engines in test-bed conditions

We have above an example of a bad graph. Graphs are read
upwards, but the natural tendency of the eye is to read from
left to right. The vertical rectangles of the grid lead the eye
upwards to the unused and wasted space at the top of this graph.

But the informative part is below this space. The effort to pack too much information on to the graph gives it a cluttered appearance which confuses the reader. British and metric units on the same graph muddle the information, as the litres/100 km scale on the right shows. The legend at the bottom should distinguish the compared curves, and the minimum of writing should appear on the grid. The arrows add insult to injury.

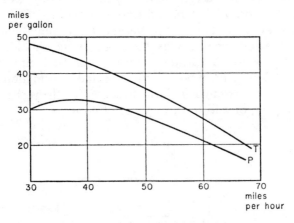

Figure 2 Fuel consumption at constant speeds of petrol engine in top gear (P) and of turbocharged diesel engine (T)

This is an example of a good graph. The curves occupy as much space on the graph as they can. Only essential information is given. The horizontal appearance makes the graph more easily read.

5.5 Illustration

Probably the two most common forms of illustration that the report writer will use are charts and line drawings.

Charts are normally useful in the co-ordination in graphic form of facts which are too numerous to be carried in the memory and which cannot be stated in words except in a long, repetitive and boring list. Such facts can, however, be displayed, and their relationships easily grasped, if they are presented on a chart used as a visual aid. And that, of course, is what a chart is for: to give instantly understandable information. The kind of information most usefully given on a chart is that of the lead-in times for assemblies and subassemblies of the production of one-off orders, especially when the contract is a large one; or that for flows of production; or that of critical pathway analysis; or that of some other kinds of production control.

Line drawings and diagrams are normally useful again as a sort of visual aid. Again, they usually display relationships. They show how parts can interact with one another, or differences in two sorts of design, or the possible arrangement of parts, or sometimes as part of an explanation of how something works.

In preparing line drawings, the report writer should, as with every other kind of illustration, always consider their usefulness to the readers of his report. Only essential information should be given. Unless drawings clarify in some way the verbal matter of the report, or add to it, they are of no use.

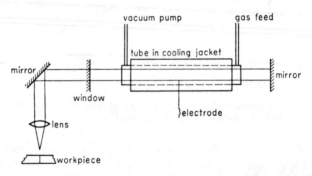

Figure 3 Diagram of arrangement of optical system for laser cutting beam focused on workpiece.

Simple line diagrams can be used to show relationships of parts, and sometimes they can help with explanations. The diagram above shows the way in which a laser beam used for cutting is focused on the material to be cut. Since the tube itself is nearly five yards long and encased in a jacket containing water, it cannot be moved, and the cutting is done by moving the workpiece in relation to the beam, and not the beam in relation to the workpiece.

The line work should, in the first stage, be roughly sketched with pencil, and several such sketches should be made, so that the report writer can visualize more accurately what he sees in his mind's eye when he conceives of the necessity for the drawing. When he has chosen that sketch which he thinks will best convey the information he wants to convey to his readers, he should draw it more carefully. The next stage would then be to pass on this drawing to those in the specialist art draughting department and consult with a draughtsman about what is really wanted. The report writer should undertake the job himself only if he is very good at drawing or there is no one else to do it for him.

All drawings should have captions, stating what they are drawings of, and may have lettering round them naming parts. The letters and symbols should be drawn with stencils, because freehand drawing, no matter how good, never has the consistency or good appearance, and not always the clarity, of stencilled work. Roman (vertical) lettering is recommended, not italics. The size of the lettering should be large enough to be legible, but not so large that it obscures and overwhelms the drawing. Lettering and annotation should be kept to a minimum. As with graphs, if the drawing cannot speak for itself, there is no need for it.

If the work is to be reproduced by photocopying or printing, it should be done in indian ink on white board.

Sometimes, of course, drawings produced in the drawing offices may be an integral part of the report, and it may be, sometimes, within the report writer's terms of reference to get them from there.

Other kinds of drawings may be maps or plans. These should normally be obtained from the experts who prepare them. Occasionally, a sketch-map of some area or site may be produced by the report writer himself; and if this is the case, the drawing should be carefully done, properly to scale, and with measurements and directions clearly indicated.

Photographs may sometimes be useful, sometimes, perhaps, even necessary. If they are necessary, the job of preparing them should be left to a professional photographer. The report writer should consult with him on all points, and should make clear exactly what the picture is intended to show and why. Sometimes the artistic feelings of the photographer and his professional desire to get a good picture may interfere with the report writer's intentions. A photograph may be of no use unless it shows the size of the object photographed; some sort of scale should therefore be introduced. Very often a photograph can be improved if something extraneous in it is got rid of. The enlargement, when it is being printed, of only a portion of the negative may sometimes be of more communicative value to the readers of the report than the whole picture.

Appendix one:
Fact Finding and Libraries

Every report writer has to have sources of information. He needs to know how to seek out facts, how to learn quickly a little more than he already knows about some topic that may be presented to him, how to check and verify the facts which he collects, how to evaluate them, how to find out what other people have said about them, and how to do all this quickly and efficiently.

He must, of course, have his own personal sources of information, always readily available in his office, laboratory, or wherever he works. In the course of his work as a writer, he will need a good dictionary, and some such reference books as Fowler's *Modern English Usage* or Partridge's *Usage and Abusage*, to which he can refer when he needs guidance on some point of English grammar or style. He should learn his way about such books as these by browsing through them, reading bits here and there, and finding out exactly how they work. And in the course of his technological and scientific duties, he will normally collect books, pamphlets, brochures, standards specifications, journals or articles from journals in the form of offprints, all of which relate to his particular discipline. He should also have some easily understood system of classifying and arranging all this material, so that he can find whatever he wants at a moment's notice.

In addition, the report writer should visit libraries and become acquainted with the wealth of information and material which most of them can nowadays offer. He should spend odd moments of his spare time in libraries so that he can learn something of the

Dewey Decimal Classification System—the one most often used in the British Commonwealth and America. He can also find out what kinds of reference books are available, what periodicals the library obtains, and what special material it may have.

In general, the report writer needs to be aware of (1) reference material, (2) special library services, (3) periodical literature, and (4) specifications.

Reference Material

By the expression *reference material* is meant encyclopaedias, dictionaries, handbooks, directories, year books, atlases, reviews of progress, and abstracts. This material can be very extensive, even in a quite small library, and it can supply all kinds of information from the torsional yield stress of carbon anodes to the cost of sending a postcard to Abu Dhabi. In order to find out how extensive this material can be, the report writer should look at the reference sections of whatever libraries he can easily reach. He should also consult a book called *Guide to Reference Material*, by A. J. Walford and L. M. Payne, published by The Library Association.

Dictionaries, of course, are the most obvious kinds of reference books. Those of us who live in the English-speaking world are fortunate in having in the *Oxford English Dictionary* the most comprehensive dictionary ever published for any language. But the *Shorter Oxford Dictionary* is generally useful for most purposes, while the *Concise Oxford Dictionary* should be the report writer's own possession always available on his desk. For American usages *Webster's New International Dictionary* should be consulted. The report writer should also be aware of *Chambers's Technical Dictionary*. There are also some specialist technical and scientific dictionaries, published by Elsevier in Europe and van Nostrand in the United States, for separate disciplines. The Elsevier dictionaries have the advantage of being multi-lingual.

Encyclopaedias can give more detailed information than dictionaries. The report writer should look at the *Encyclopaedia Britannica* and *Chambers's Encyclopaedia*, so that he can become familiar with the kinds of information that they may be able to supply for him. Useful summaries, definitions, and a vast amount of scientific and technical knowledge, with most articles furnished with ample cross-references, can also be found in *The McGraw-Hill Encyclopaedia of Science and Technology*.

In recent years, several handbooks giving reviews of progress in different specialist fields have become available. Such are *Progress in Automation*, published by Butterworth, London, or *Advances in Applied Mechanics*, published by the Academic Press, also in London, or the *Annual Report on Progress in Chemistry*, published by the Chemical Society.

It is impossible, in the course of a short appendix, to give details of all the vast quantities of reference material that is now available. But librarians are approachable people; their job is to know what kinds of information can be found; and they are used to answering all sorts of queries, from the most trivial to those of —at least for the writer—epoch-making importance.

Special Library Services

In addition to the public libraries maintained by local authorities, and the private libraries of universities and colleges, there are several special libraries and information services. These special libraries and information services are normally in the reach of most public libraries, and the use of them is either free or can be obtained on subscription.

One of these is the Patents Office Library in London, which has a vast collection of scientific and technological literature and a vast, indeed unique, collection of literature about patents.

Another special library service is that provided by the National Lending Library for Science and Technology at Boston Spa in Yorkshire. This library can lend through other libraries an enormous amount of scientific and technical literature; it has the merit of providing an exceptionally quick service.

In recent years several local information services, available for research and industry, have been growing in importance. These are based on the libraries of some local centres. Some provide a service to subscribing members; others are free. One of the earliest to come into existence was HERTIS, which is based on the library of Hatfield College of Technology, and to which industrial and research organizations can subscribe. Another is CICRIS, based on the Acton Public Library, and is a co-operative information service including municipal, college and industrial libraries in West London. Others are LETIS, based on the Leicester City Library, NANTIS, based on Nottingham, HULTIS, based on Hull, and LADSIRIAC, based on the City Library of Liverpool. Information about any of these special services, and all others, can be obtained from any public library.

ASLIB, or the Association of Special Libraries and Information Bureaux, is a national organization with regional centres which serves subscribing members. It deals with a large number of industrial inquiries, research information, provides a book loan service, a panel of translators of scientific and technical literature from and into most languages, and has a good index of translations. The ASLIB Directory is useful for those who want to know the whereabouts of special and out-of-the-way reference material.

Periodical Literature

Such a vast amount of scientific and technological material is nowadays published in periodical form that it is quite impossible for any one man to know all that is happening even in his own specialist field. Nevertheless, the report writer should know what means there are for finding one's way about.

The *British National Bibliography*, which started publication in 1950, is a weekly list of almost all books published in Great Britain. There is a monthly cumulated index giving authors, titles and subjects. Quarterly and annual volumes are also published. The *British National Bibliography* can be consulted at almost any library, and certainly at all public libraries, for it is one of the essential tools of the librarian's profession.

Willing's Press Guide is an annual publication which gives information about newspapers, magazines, journals and periodicals published in Great Britain and the Irish Republic, as well as about the chief periodicals of the Commonwealth. *Ulrich's Periodicals Directory*, published every three years by the R. R. Bowker Company of New York, lists thousands of periodicals from all over the world.

The Library Association publishes the *British Technology Index,* which is an extremely useful guide to the subject-matter of articles published in scientific and technological journals in Great

Britain. It is issued monthly, and there is an annual cumulated volume.

Every report writer will soon become aware of the periodical literature relating to his own discipline. Much of the material found in periodicals is now abstracted, so that those who are interested can search through the abstracts to find what they want, without having to try to undertake the enormous and impossible task of reading everything. The report writer will soon learn how to use whatever abstracts he needs; he will see that the abstract gives bibliographic information about the whereabouts of the article in question, and a short précis of the subject-matter so that the reader can decide whether it will be useful for him to look up the original article or not. Examples of such abstracts are *Chemical Abstracts*, issued by the American Chemical Society, or *Metallurgical Abstracts*, issued by the Institute of Metals, or the *Electrical Engineering Abstracts*, issued by the Institution of Electrical Engineers, or the *Index Aeronautics*, issued by the Ministry of Aviation. There are also a few specialized abstracts on various subjects issued by the Department of Scientific and Industrial Research.

Specifications

Every report writer will have sooner or later in his dealings with scientific and technological subjects to refer to a specification of some kind of material or product, or to the codes or practice used in manufacture, assemblies, structures or testing. In Britain, the British Standards Institution deals with all matters relating to the standards and specifications of recommended properties of materials, dimensions, limits, and approved methods of testing. The report writer should consult the *British Standards Yearbook*— making sure he has the current one, for standards and specifications are frequently revised. The *BSI News* is a monthly publication which provides information about new standards and specifications as they are issued.

Appendix two:
An Editorial Section

Thousands of the reports which are written every day are merely routine and *ad hoc* pieces of writing that are of no interest or value once their immediate aim has been achieved. Each is useful in getting a job done, but once that job is finished, no one wants to be bothered with the report that helped.

However, many firms nowadays have research departments. The amount of money annually made available for research, both publicly and privately, now makes these departments of supreme importance to industry. The main work of such departments is not in direct participation in the tasks of converting raw materials into the firm's products, but in the thinking and scientific and technological principles behind such tasks. The research departments produce reports which are not only of interest to top management and technical management, but also to customers, to sub-contractors and suppliers of materials, to firms within the same group, to firms with allied interests, and to other research organizations.

Reports such as these need careful and expert handling. The job of looking after the preparation of reports of such high quality is best left to a special editorial or publications section. And the work of such a section should not be confused with that of the publications departments of some firms. The section dealing with reports is not the same as that dealing with handbooks, parts lists, maintenance manuals, catalogues or publicity literature. It should be a separate and autonomous organization and should deal with nothing but the processing and control of reports. If the section is, for administrative convenience, housed with or under the control of some such officer as a publications manager, its separateness should be clearly defined, and the personnel of the section should not, ideally, be called upon to deal with the production of general publications.

The chief officer of such a section is an editor. Under his control are as many assistant editors as the section needs. Also under his control are some art draughtsmen or draughtswomen who are capable of understanding technical illustration and the problems of presenting ideas graphically. The editor and his assistants also need secretarial help, and their typists should not, in ideal circumstances, be drawn from a general typing pool, but should be looked upon as having special secretarial qualifications for their work on research reports.

The qualifications needed by the editor and his assistants are hard to define. To speak generally, men of broad scientific or technological background who also have a talent for writing make the best kind of editors. One such editor, a highly successful man at his job, employed in the aircraft industry, told the writer of this book that the ideal editor would be a scientist or engineer who had failed to make good in science or engineering, because his failure to make good might be put down to his ability to be objective. Another such editor, also highly successful, employed in an internationally known research organization dealing with light alloys, told the writer that the ideal editor needed the same type of mind as a good computer programmer—he should be an artist who never showed temperament and never allowed his feelings to interfere with his work. Certainly, a good editor needs objectivity, patience, a tactful firmness in dealing with people, and a sympathetic flair for seeing other people's problems and difficulties without becoming involved with them.

The work of the section will be the receiving of draft reports and the production of them in the correct form for internal and external presentation. Perhaps the flow of work can be understood from Figure 1.

The aim of the editorial section is to relieve those engaged in the actual research of as much as possible of the literary side of report writing, to control the processing of reports, and to keep a record of what report writing has been done. There are other

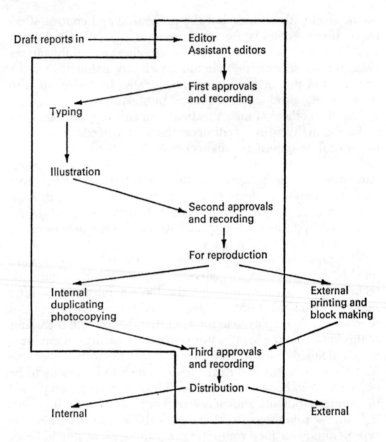

Figure 1 Diagram of the flow of work in a research report editorial section

apparently minor duties that may fall to the editor and his assistants. They may have to prepare a style manual or handbook for report writers; they might issue regular news sheets; and they might publish some periodical review, a printed and often glossy document, which gives prestige to the firm or group of companies and at the same time provides useful and interesting information about the kind of work the firm and its applied companies are engaged in, or about the thinking behind such work. The editor should also keep a continual surveillance over the policy and development of the section. He may also have to prepare periodical reports about the section's own activities and

Report No... Dead line.....................

Title ....

Author/s ....

.... Dept/Section....................

Classification .... Authorization...................

Destination .... Internal/External

Editing

Draft received	....	Checked	....
Typed	....	"	....
Edited	....	"	....
First Approvals	....	"	....
Second "	....	"	....
Third "	....	"	....

Remarks ....

....

Reproduction

Main text	....	Ordered	....
....		Checked	....
Graphs	....	Ordered	....
....		Checked	....
Drawings	....	Ordered	....
....		Checked	....
Photographs	....	Ordered	....
....		Checked	....
Printing	....	Ordered	....
....		Checked	....
Covers	....	Ordered	....
....		Checked	....

Copies ordered ....

Assembled ....

Passed for distribution .... Checked.....................

Figure 2 Suggested form of record sheet which should go with a report
during its career in the editorial section

present them to those in authority. Sometimes, too, the section may have to exercise some financial control, or at least some elementary book-keeping, of work such as printing, photographing or translation which it may commission externally.

The work of editing consists of setting a draft manuscript in order, checking and if necessary revising the English, preparing any graphs or illustrations that may be wanted, and seeing to the preparation and reproduction of the report in its final form. There may also, in some research organizations, arise the need for abstracting and the translation of abstracts into foreign languages—chiefly German, French and Spanish. These abstracts are then printed along with the report. Translators for such work can usually be found outside the organization, and are employed on a part-time basis.

The control and organization of the work of an editorial section may be seen by comparing and collating the ideas given in Figures 1 and 2. Figure 2 gives a suggested form or a record sheet which should accompany every report during its passage through the editorial section.

The moment the draft report is received some such record sheet should be made out for it. Most important is the dead line. This is the date by which the finished report must be ready. How far ahead of the date of the receipt of the draft that deadline date will be is a question that can be answered only by experience. Sometimes the author who sends in the draft may fix the date; very often he will be optimistic. But the editor or one of his assistants, as he fills up the record sheet, will become aware of what has to be done—whether the report is for internal or external use, whether it will take only a few hours or several days to have it properly typed, whether the graphs or illustrations can be prepared quickly or not, whether work already in hand can be dispatched easily or will cause delays, and so on. One fact is clear. That is that the quality of a report depends on the time and care given to it. If the job is rushed, it will not be a job well done. The dead line should be fixed at a date which will give everybody ample time to do his work properly. Once the dead line has been fixed it should be binding upon everybody concerned.

Since the record sheet is both a statement of what is to be done and a progress report, all the entries to be made on it cannot, of course, be made immediately. But it can provide an estimate of the amount of work that the particular report it accompanies entails.

The word *approvals* as used in Figures 1 and 2 is one that covers a number of different activities. When the record sheet is filled in as much as it can be immediately after the draft is received, it shows what is to be done—how many graphs and drawings are needed, how the main text is to be reproduced, whether duplicated or printed, for example, and how many copies are to be ordered. As soon as this is estimated, the work of doing it has to be allocated to the people who are going to do it. Dates for finishing the various jobs can be set to occur between the date of receipt of the draft and the date of the dead line.

All this information can then be reproduced on a wall chart or progress indicator. One useful type of progress indicator is a frame with paper board pockets into which slips of card can be inserted. Titles across the top of the frame give the names of the jobs to be done, and the pocket under each title can have a coloured card bearing the estimated date put in it. As soon as the particular job is finished, a card of a different colour bearing the date of finishing is put in the place of the original one. Thus progress can be seen at a glance, and at any stage those in the editorial section know where any report is and what work has been done on it. At the same time, as soon as a particular job is finished, the person who finishes it, or who is responsible for seeing that it is finished, initials the appropriate space after the word *Checked* on the record sheet.

The first approvals, therefore, will include these jobs of estimating what has to be done, and allocating the different parts of the work to those people who have to do it.

However, before the actual preparation of the report in its final form can get under way, the text has to be edited and the illustrative material examined. The report cannot be prepared for final presentation until the personnel of the editorial section know exactly what it is they have to prepare.

First, the report has to be typed, if it is not already typed when it comes from the hands of the author. And even if the author does send in his draft already typed, he may not be a good typist, he may have made several or many corrections, and the copy may not be 'clean', that is, not in a good state for the editorial work to begin.

Ideally, the editorial section should have its own standards of presentation of typed material. There should be standard sizes of paper, standard type faces, standard margin widths, a standard number of lines to a page, and so on. Attention to such matters as these can make it easy to estimate the length of material, the number of words in a report, and can also make it easy for the personnel of the section to find their way about among headings, spacing, parts of the report, layout, and so on.

With a good clean copy in front of him, the editor can begin his work. We have stressed in this book that reports are written to be read, and that the writer should always try to think of the reader. This is the point of view from which the editor should look at the report he is editing. He will try to put himself in the place of the eventual reader, and thus make an effort to be objective. He will try to grasp the author's theme, to evaluate the points which the author wants to make, and to appreciate the significance of all the parts of the report and the ways in which they contribute to the effect of the whole. He may then, when it comes to details, make suggestions about paragraphing and the relationships of paragraphs to one another, as well as about points of style and usage. But even if there is a house style, the editor should not attempt to change the author's style fundamentally, though he may believe that some changes ought to be made to make an explanation more clear, a description more vivid, or to reduce wordiness, or correct grammar. If the editor believes that there are errors of fact in the report, he should make a note of them.

When all this has been done, the editor should bring to the notice of the author any changes that he proposes to make, and he should explain why he thinks that they are needed. This consultation with authors may sometimes be a trying business, for all authors are fond of their children and have an irritating propensity of often believing that they are right and everybody else is wrong. However, the wise author will always listen carefully to what the editor has to say, since the editor can always be more objective and, seeing the work from a different point of view, can often anticipate adverse criticisms and difficulties of readers. Certainly, the editor should try to earn for himself the reputation of being respected and acknowledged as an expert at his job. In his consultations with authors he will need all his tact, patience and professional expertise. And in matters of English usage, grammar, style and presentation, the editor's word should be final.

At the same time as he discusses the proposed changes in the main text with the author, the editor should also discuss graphs and illustrations. He should be able to assess the author's needs, be able to point out to the author exactly what illustrations can do for the report, and he may indeed sometimes suggest that a table, a graph or a drawing could be used when the author has not thought of supplying one.

The first approvals, then, should be the culmination of all this work. The typed copy of the main text, properly edited, with a clear idea of what kind and how many graphs and illustrations are to be used, should then be available for the report's first presentation.

The round of activities leading to the second approvals will be preparing the main text for reproduction, ordering the graphs and illustrations, and making sure that all these are ready and assembled together by the date set on the progress indicator. If the work leading to the first approvals has been done well, this next round of activities should go fairly smoothly; in a well organized editorial section it can even become routine.

When this work is finished, the report should be ready for reproduction. The record sheet that belongs to it will by this time have considerably fewer blank spaces. The second approval is indeed nothing more than a thorough check that the work initiated by the first approvals has been done properly and that nothing has been missed.

The round of activities leading to the third approvals should, in most cases, be very simple. The work has merely to be reproduced. If the report in its final stage has merely to be duplicated for internal use, there is no very real difficulty. The typed and edited copy can be transferred to stencils, and all that is necessary is to check the stencils before they are run off. If the report has to be printed, the same sort of checking will have to be done on the proofs as they come from the printer.

The third approvals will be the examination and checking of everything before it is passed for distribution. It should be very unlikely at this stage that anything has gone wrong. Any snags or difficulties should have been discovered and put right or overcome during the round of activities after the second approvals. But it never does any harm to give a final check, just in case.

One task that the editorial section should perform after every report that passes through its hands has been distributed, is keep a record of its activities. The information, or some of it, on the record sheet of each report should be transferred to a card in a card indexing system, so that some kind of memorial of the activities of the section remains. Perhaps, in some establishments, this card could carry an abstract of the report.

Index